Unstuck

Acclaim for *Unstuck* by Cara Brookins

"Whether you're ready to climb a mountain or knock one down, Unstuck delivers your strategy for success!"
—Alison Levine, History-making adventurer and New York Times bestselling author of *On the Edge*

"When executives and sales professionals fail to reach their goals, it's often because they or their team are stuck without a plan. This uplifting book is filled with stories that illustrate a powerful, sensible formula to deliver tremendous success."
—Ian Altman - Bestselling co-author, *Same Side Selling* and Founder SameSideSellingAcademy.com

"Cara Brookins' determined, innovative use of how-to videos is motivation for anyone who has ever pressed pause when they should have pressed play.

I have to confess, when we began YouTube in the garages of Menlo Park, I never thought that the future reality would be meeting an extraordinary person like Cara, connected via the YouTube service!"
—Steve Chen, original co-founder of YouTube

"We all get stuck. When it happens to you, use *Unstuck* as your how-to guide for what to do next."
—Brian Levenson, Executive Coach and Author of *Shift Your Mind*

"If you've ever been paralyzed by doubt, indecision, uncertainty, and fear, take hold of Cara Brookins' hand and let her walk you through the solution, one how-to video strategy at a time.

With equal parts warmth, wit, and wisdom, Unstuck will show you the way to reach the biggest goal possible. All you need to do is press play!"
　—Laura Gassner Otting, bestselling author of *Wonderhell*

"Unstuck is a charming and practical masterpiece in tackling life's goals. This book rocks!"
　—Jim Knight, keynote speaker, bestselling author of *Culture That Rocks*, part-time procrastinator

"In Unstuck, Cara Brookins delivers laugh-out-loud examples of how to engage the most stubborn parts of your brain and then use them to accomplish your biggest goals."
　—Marc A. Pitman, author of *The Surprising Gift of Doubt*

Unstuck

END PROCRASINATION USING
THE ANCIENT PSYCHOLOGY
BEHIND HOW-TO VIDEOS

CARA BROOKINS

UNSTUCK

End Procrastination Using the Ancient Psychology Behind How-to Videos

Copyright © 2023 by Cara Brookins. All rights reserved. Printed in the United States of America. No part of this book may be reproduced or used in any manner without the prior written permission of the copyright owner. To request permissions, contact By Brookins, Inc. at cara@carabrookins.com www.carabrookins.com

Cover Designed by Young Lim and Hope Brookins
Photographs by Sarah Oden
Edited by Mari Farthing

979-8-9872859-1-6 (hardcover)
979-8-9872859-0-9 (paperback)
979-8-9872859-8-5 (ebook)
979-8-9872859-9-2 (audiobook)

Library of Congress Control Number: 2023904163

Our books may be purchased in bulk for promotional, educational, or business use. Please contact your local bookseller or the By Brookins, Inc Corporate and Premium Sales Department at cara@carabrookins.com
Bryant, Arkansas

First edition March 2023
10 9 8 7 6 5 4 3 2 1

To my daughter Hope Brookins who was flooded with
endless details as I researched this book.
But she still listened, advised, and read every word nearly
as many times as I did.

I'm so proud of who you are and all you do.

Table of Contents

Introduction	1
Chapter One – I'm Stuck	11
Chapter Two – Fight, Flight, or Freeze	31
Chapter Three – The Press Play Effect	49
Chapter Four – Set The Scene	68
Chapter Five – Action	86
Chpater Six – Rewind	106
Chapter Seven – Worst Case Scenario	126
Chapter Eight – The Yet Principle	147
Chapter Nine – The Last Person on Earth	167
Chapter Ten – The Quit Early Effect	186
Chapter Eleven – Troubleshooting	203
Chapter Twelve – Your Goal Play Button	221
Quick Reference	227
Lemon Bundt Cake Recipe	233
Acknowledgements	235
References	239

Introduction

THE BEGINNING IS THE MOST IMPORTANT
PART OF THE WORK. - PLATO

It's 2019 and my agent has been relentlessly pressuring me to write my next book, but I don't have a topic. I've been speaking at events all over the world, looking for my book topic at every stop. On a Thursday afternoon in North Platte, Nebraska, I step onto the stage of a gorgeous restored theater. A thousand people have come out in the middle of a Thursday to discuss my memoir *Rise*, about how I built my own house with my four kids using how-to videos.

When the audience begins asking questions, I spot a theme. One person after another says, "I feel stuck."

For some, the feeling began when they changed careers, or lost someone they loved. Others said it came out of nowhere, or when they finally arrived at the biggest opportunity of their life. Instantly, they felt stuck with no idea what to do next.

I knew right then that I had my topic. Because I had been stuck too, and I had found a way to get myself unstuck, over and over again.

You probably already guessed that I learned my unstuck strategy while building my house, but the way it started may surprise you. It began on a chilly fall evening in 2007 when every part of my life was a mess, until I accidentally baked a cake. And because nothing happens the way we expect it to, that small cake ended up changing my life in big ways.

To be honest, I'd rather tell you the whole thing happened while I was reading the classics or meditating with a renowned guru or something. But, nope.

A lemon Bundt cake changed my life.

I know, you're thinking: An epiphany over cake batter? Please, spare me the drama and give me the recipe. But the actual dramatic moment had nothing to do with flour, egg shells, or even the fluffy, rich end result. It was all about the second I decided to take the first step. A step that began as a tiny fire in my brain that moved me from sitting at my computer to instantly springing up to bake a cake.

Because that's what this book is about. It's about finding the thing that will get you to take a step toward whatever project or goal you should be springing up to work on right now. It's about how sometimes we feel so stuck in place that we don't know how to begin. And it's about how we can end that cycle forever.

This book will get you moving.

That's right, this book is the link between where you are now, and where you want to be. Because standing in my kitchen on that Tuesday in 2007, I discovered an important secret—and I've been cooking up big goals ever since.

I'm the first to admit I had absolutely no business baking a cake when I had a million other things to focus on—my finances were a disaster, my family relationships were suffering in every way, my career had flatlined, and worst of all I was about to lose the house I was living in with my four kids. Literally anything I could have been doing that night would have made more sense than that cake. And here's what's even weirder about that.

I wasn't planning to bake anything that night, or even that week. A lemon Bundt cake wasn't something I'd ever considered making in my life. This was truly, in every way, an accidental baking. If that sounds weirdly impossible, I get it. But when you hear how it happened, I bet you'll say, "Oh, yeah. That's happened to me lots of times, too."

What I was doing is sitting at my computer alternating between email cleanup and searching for side-jobs. I'd already eaten dinner, and even though I didn't have any sort of dessert, I hadn't missed it in the least. Then, out of nowhere, a how-to video popped up that began with some guy holding up a perfectly beautiful cake. He said (in the overenergized voice of all YouTubers), "We're going to bake your new favorite cake *right now* in three easy steps."

I was skeptical.

But then he looked me straight in the eye and took a bite of that cake, and something happened to me. I could taste lemon on my tongue and my mouth watered, and there was nothing I wanted more at that moment in life than a lemon Bundt cake.

I didn't pause to consider if this was the best use of my time. I didn't search my calendar for a cake-worthy event. I didn't even do a calorie count. I stood up, walked to my kitchen, and I baked that cake.

At first this probably sounds like a big so-what moment. I get it. In that instant I didn't realize either that anything more profound was going on than the incredible smell of warm, sugary lemons. In fact, by the time I sat back at my computer and ate my first bite of that lemony cake, I felt a little silly about the way I'd spent my night.

Then, when I least expected, the whole thing happened again.

I was still chewing that first warm bite of lemon cake with the perfect mix of sweet and tart when another video popped up. How to replace your laptop battery. And there I was, an old laptop flipped over on the desk next to my warm cake—fork in one hand and screw driver in the other.

What was happening to me?

At a time when I felt completely stuck, too paralyzed to get myself out of a single one of the massive problems I was facing, I was suddenly and unexpectedly springing into action on projects that minutes before I had absolutely no intention of doing—projects that at first glance had nothing to do with each other.

That's when it hit me. The projects did have one thing in common after all. They had been launched by a how-to video.

Had those how-to videos hypnotized me? Had they

seized control of my brain? Hacked into my actions? Whatever was going on, these videos pulled me up and got me moving in a way I hadn't been able to get myself up and moving. And whether you like cake or disassembling electronic devices or not, that's something worth thinking about. I had a feeling I could use the strange pull from these videos to do something even bigger. But in that moment, I had no idea what that might be.

I brushed off the feeling—and the cake crumbs—and I went to bed. But the next morning at five o'clock while I was taking a shower (where all great ideas are born, am I right?), I couldn't stop thinking about what had happened. That's when I started to unravel what those videos had done to me.

Those how-to videos had instantly pulled me up to do something without requiring me to understand the whole process first.

They had moved me so quickly from a what-if idea to a countertop covered in egg shells and flour that I didn't have time to resist. And that got me thinking.

If I could set up one of my goals, a thing that really mattered, in the same way the how-to videos had set up a cake. Then I could start anything with that same high level of confidence.

It would be like setting up a goal with a built-in play button. The only thing I'd have to do to succeed is press play.

The effect of that realization was huge—life-changing even. I had come across a lot of cake recipes in my life. In fact, the cabinet to the left of my oven had a huge stack that I'd cut out from magazines and printed from blogs, thinking that I'd bake them someday. Of course, someday never arrived for those cakes. And never, not once in my entire life, had I read the title of a recipe in print or online and instantly stood up to go make it. Something new and different had been unlocked by the format of those how-to videos, and I was determined to figure out how it worked.

I wasn't sure in that moment all the ways a simple two-minute video could influence my mind and behavior, but I figured I didn't have to know every last detail in order to use what I understood about it at first glance. The success clearly had something to do with how quickly the video got me moving on my goal. Could I possibly put a thing like that to use?

Well, a whole lot of things were wrong in my life, so I took a close look at how I was approaching them. I realized that every single time I had an idea for something that might improve things, I ended up spouting off a long list of reasons I couldn't or shouldn't make those moves yet. Things like: *I should wait for more money, more skill, more time, or more resources.* Or things like: *I should wait for less stress, less doubt, or just less on my plate.*

If I had to declare my theme for that year it would have (embarrassingly) been something like: *She thought she couldn't or she shouldn't—so she didn't.*

But that morning in the shower, I decided to do things differently. I decided that when my next idea hit, instead of pressing pause while I waited for more or less of something, I would instead spring into action. I'd tackle that next idea exactly like I had tackled that cake video. I wouldn't let it matter that I didn't understand the whole process. I would immediately get up and do the first step, and then I would just keep pressing play.

Of course, I had no idea in that moment what my next project idea would be. (Boy was I in for a surprise.) But I did know that time was running out for me to improve things for me and for my kids. I had felt stuck for far too long. And I knew that the key to getting unstuck was somehow related to this idea of jolting myself into that first step. I was convinced that after I had the momentum of that first step, I could just figure out the rest as I went.

And I didn't simply imagine that was true, I had watched it happen with the cake and the laptop battery. One step at a time, I figured out how to do both of those things even though I'd never done them before. I started calling the effect those videos had on me the "press play" effect, because I was compelled to take action mere seconds after I pressed play.

With a new-found confidence that I could recreate this self-starting effect in my own life, I stepped out of that shower and got the kids ready for school. Not twenty minutes later, hair still wet from that shower as I drove the kids to school, I had an idea for a project that would change our lives forever.

"We need a house," I whispered out loud to myself at a traffic light.

Now it wasn't the first time I realized we needed a safe place to live. It wasn't even the first time I'd brainstormed how to solve that problem. But it was the first time that I immediately sprung to action on the first step. That small shift in the way I approached my goal changed everything.

I bought the land, secured a construction loan and began building.

I kept figuring out the next steps. And over the next nine months, my kids and I built a house with our own hands. And we built it using the same system that had first jolted me to action in that *how-to bake a lemon Bundt cake* video. It began with that idea of taking a quick blind action, but I learned right away that that was only a small part of why these short videos packed such a big punch. Each how-to video was packed full of brain hacks that I could implement every day.

Later, sitting at my desk in that finished house, I watched thousands of how-to videos and studied how each technique got me unstuck.

What I found were a handful of tried-and-true success methods that were definitely not created by YouTubers. In fact, these methods have been used by successful people throughout history. I found a handful of subtle differences in the way the how-to videos used them though, things that elevated the success rate, things that made that all-important first action feel not only possible but irresistible.

To my surprise, these simple videos were using the best psychological tricks in the best ways and packaging them all together into a bite-sized moment. This incredible discovery just kept getting better.

I kept using the method behind these how-to videos to perfect the way I set up my own projects, and it kept working.

Which brings me to why I'm writing this book.

After I built my house, I published eight books (nine since you're reading this), started a successful speaking business, and optioned my life story for film, reality TV, and a limited TV series. Because of this, people have sent me thousands of notes from all over the world that boil down to one universal statement:

I know my life can be better than it is today. I know I'm capable of so much more. But I just feel stuck. **How do I take the next step?**

That, my friend, is exactly how I felt on that chilly fall evening in 2007 when I accidentally baked a cake. That night I learned that how-to videos aren't just a shortcut to your new favorite dessert, they're a shortcut to your biggest success. That lemon Bundt cake was more than a diversion—it was the first step of the next chapter of my life.

If you feel stuck in one small part of your life, or even if the whole mess feels stuck at once, I understand how you feel. No matter how long you pull and tug with all your strength to break free from that stuck feeling, you wake up just as stuck today as yesterday.

It turns out, the solution is exactly like one of those ancient bamboo finger traps. Remember those novelty toys? A finger trap is just a finger-sized woven straw, but when you put a finger in each end and pull, the straw gets tighter and tighter the harder you tug. This little toy is deceptively simple, just relax and lean in to get free. But even after you know how it works, your heart races over how useless your resistance is. It's the opposite of everything you think should be true. Because the harder you try, the more stuck you feel. Sound familiar?

I found a way to get unstuck and succeed at the goals in my life. And now I want you to feel that success in your life and your business, too.

Are you ready? Let's do this together.

All you have to do is press play.

CHAPTER ONE

I'm Stuck

YOU DON'T HAVE TO BE GREAT TO START, BUT YOU HAVE TO START TO BE GREAT.

- ZIG ZIGLAR

In 1966, a man in India decided there should be a road between his small village and a nearby town with schools, markets, and a hospital. He wasn't the first one to be cut and bruised on the narrow mountain path, or to curse the fifty mile walk that was the only route to medicine and supplies. He wasn't the first person to wish the mountain between himself and sometimes life-saving services would disappear.

He *was* the first to pick up a hammer, chisel, and shovel and start chipping away.

Of course everyone laughed at him. They said it was

impossible for a man to move a mountain.

But Dashrath Manjhi got up every day with his primitive tools and carried away a few more pieces of the mountain. And he did this nearly every day for twenty-two years.

When asked what the first days of this work were like, Manjhi said, "When I started hammering the hill, people called me a lunatic but that steeled my resolve."

And his resolve was extraordinary.

By 1988, he had reduced the distance from his village to the neighboring resources from fifty miles to under two miles. Supplies, medicine, and hospitals that once took days to reach were now a short walk away. The children could attend school. Manjhi was celebrated in the village and then across the country. He was even honored on postage stamps, and his story became a film in 2015.

One single man faced a common problem and did an uncommon thing. One single man moved a mountain.

Here's the most important question: Why did he begin?

On a day that was for all appearances exactly the same as any other day, why did he get up and do something completely unconventional?

Why did he take the first step?

The answer changes everything.

Because once you know the answer to that question, you can do the same thing. You can get up today and do something completely unconventional. You can have an idea and immediately take action. You can take *your* first step. And that means, just like Manjhi, you can accomplish extraordinary things.

You can move mountains.

What Makes You Feel Stuck

It probably seems like there are dozens, even hundreds of reasons why only one person in the entire village decided to move the mountain. Or why Manjhi decided to begin on that day in 1966 and none of the days before that. Or even why today one person decides to paint their dining room on Friday night and is finished by Sunday at lunch time, while another across town has been tripping over the new paint cans for a year, and still another has used the paint swatch options as drink coasters for so long that they don't even remember why they have those paint swatches in the first place.

But the reasons you have trouble taking a step forward aren't complex at all. They're actually very simple. The pathway in your brain that takes you directly from a great idea into an endless loop of feeling stuck is a universal pathway. This is true no matter how ambitious and determined you are, no matter how intelligent, no matter how important the goal is to you. In fact, you procrastinate *because* of how efficiently your brain works. Humans are just plain wired to procrastinate.

The feeling is so universal that if you're not careful you will accept it as a personality trait instead of a problem. In fact, you may even stop trying to get unstuck. And that would be a tragedy.

To get a clear understanding of what's going on in your head when you feel stuck, let's talk about the two distinct types of situations that happen when we label ourselves as stuck.

Sneak Attack

You're moving through your normal, ordinary life, and it hits you out of nowhere. You go to work, school, events, dinners and everything is just fine. I mean life is never completely perfect, but you know what I mean. Nothing terrible or profound is happening in your life. Until one day, you just start to feel off. It's a little wiggle of a feeling at first, but it keeps building until you have this irresistible urge for something in your life to *change*.

It begins with a feeling of restless energy, but when you're not sure what to do with that energy it leads to frustration, and as the frustration builds you get the sense that your feet are stuck in the mud. You feel trapped. You don't know how to take the first step toward something better. Heck, you aren't even sure anymore what that something better is. Is that job, that goal, or that project even the thing you really want in life? The more you try to sort it all out, the less sure you are about anything.

This feeling is a lot more powerful than a gentle, "I wish…" or a casual "Wouldn't it be cool if…" or even that humble, "Someday I'd like to…" Those soft feelings are things you can be easily distracted from. If you go to a movie, grab an ice cream cone, or go for a stroll with friends, you'll forget you even felt anything was off.

What I'm talking about here is more like a summer rain that suddenly dumps on you from a single cloud in a clear blue sky. It's a day when all at once you aren't as comfortable in your own skin as you were the day before. You're just moving along and doing the same things you usually do without anything weird happening, but suddenly on this perfectly ordinary day that restless feeling rains down all over you. And no distractions will work to shift your focus away from that restlessness.

The feeling builds and grows until it feels like your skin is crawling. And the worst part is, you may not even be able to put your finger on what you'd like to change about your life. You may feel guilty for feeling dissatisfied when nothing major in your life is actually wrong right now. Still, you can't shake the feeling that you want something different, something *more*.

This feeling isn't as mysterious or complex as it may seem. In fact, it's as simple as you outgrowing your current situation. Your mind and body send that restless feeling as a prompt to get you moving toward something bigger and better. It sounds like an efficient system, like this feeling should keep you moving upward on endless ladders of self-improvement, landing in better relationships, better houses, and better careers after each restless flutter.

But often, you end up suspended in that middle ground, too uncertain to move forward and too dissatisfied where you are. No one can exist in that middle ground for long because the feeling grows from weirdly uncomfortable to maddening. It's a recipe for disaster. (Until, of course, you learn how to use these moments to make your life better, which is exactly what we're going to do.)

This sneak-attack route to feeling stuck is so common that I'm sure that every single one of us has felt it at some point in life. But it's not the only way you get stuck.

Lightning Strike

Then there's a thing that rams right into you with a major life event. We're talking the sort of thing that really turns your world upside down.

This could be any negative thing in life from a health or financial crisis, to a divorce, or losing someone close to you. This crisis doesn't have to be house-fire level big for you to feel like your world has burned down; sometimes moving to a new town or even a new house can set off a chain of negative reactions. No matter how big or small this event looks from a distance, up close your life feels like it was impacted in every single way. Traumatic events from bad circumstances or decisions hit us hard and can hold us down.

You feel stuck in a deep pit. You feel alone, uncertain, sad, even scared, and you don't know how to dig your way out of all that. Whether you're struggling to take the first step back toward your old normal life or toward something completely new, a crisis can leave you feeling completely trapped. Not only are you uncertain about which step to take, you aren't sure you'll have what it takes to move forward even after you figure that out.

Negative life events strike fast and hard, but it isn't just the bad stuff that holds us back. While you can see pretty quickly how those negative changes leave you feeling stuck, you might be surprised to learn that positive life changes can land you there, too. Things like bringing home a new baby, getting married, starting your dream job, or buying a house all sound like the answer, not like the problem. But they are often the very thing that locks our feet in place and makes us feel like everything is off kilter.

These events strike like: *BOOM*

The impact is enormous and unexpected. Even if you knew this thing was going to happen, you had no idea how big of a mark it would leave.

And there you are, scrambling to figure out how to navigate by a completely new set of rules. Somewhere in the middle of it, you may feel like you have everything under control. Whether it was a positive or negative thing that set off the chaos, you eventually learn to juggle it all pretty well. Or at the very least, you're holding it together—even if it is by a thread. But here's where everything changes.

As the whirlwind stills, that old stuck feeling nails your feet to the floor. You know it's possible to get to a better place than you're in right now. Not only have you seen other people do it, you're pretty sure you have what it takes too. If only you had some idea how to motivate yourself to take one step forward.

Day after day after week after year, you tell yourself that first step is right around the corner.

I know how frustrating it is to never reach that corner. To want the solution to hit you with the same big blast of inevitable certainty that the problem did. I have ridden the rollercoaster of optimism followed by the crushing thought that maybe I just didn't have it in me after all. I've been there. And I've also found my way out, and now you are doing the same thing.

Restlessness is an Action Prompt

One of the things that will surprise you most along the way is that these restless feelings are actually supposed to happen to you. They're supposed to make you pause. Here's the thing though, you're not supposed to pause for long. You're not supposed to freeze in place for good. You're only supposed to pause long enough to pivot toward your new path, and then you're supposed to launch forward. That's right, this stuck feeling is designed to move you to a better place. And learning to recognize not only the feeling but what you should do with it is the first step toward taking your first step.

Think about it—this restless, antsy feeling is making you uncomfortable where you are so you will move to a new spot. And that's a very good thing. I know that's a completely new way to look at the onset of a stuck feeling, but it's absolutely true and really, really important.

Look at this entire thing in this brand-new way: feeling stuck isn't the problem, staying stuck is.

Here's what I mean by that. The reason you feel stuck all boils down to one thing—you want something in your life to be different than it is, but you feel a resistance to taking the first step. See? The feeling is good. It's simply a tap on the shoulder saying, *Psst, you can do better than this*. And we can all agree we need regular reminders in life to be the best versions of ourselves.

But then comes the bad part, that resistance you feel over taking the first step toward that better thing. That resistance can come from lots of different places. Maybe you don't have the money, time, skill, or whatever you think you need right now. Maybe you're afraid you'll fail, or look ridiculous, or that people will say you're a little crazy for trying to do this thing. You may not even be able to articulate why you aren't taking that step, but still, day after day you do everything *except* the thing that will get you closer to the career, hobby, or life you want.

That's all assuming you know exactly what you want to change in your life, and maybe you do.

But sometimes this feeling hits and you don't have a clue what that first step might be. You have the motivation, and maybe even the time and money to reach your goal, but you have no idea what to do first. You're so anxious to reach your end goal that you're wiggling in your seat. You can hardly stand the suspense. But no matter how strong that urge grows, it never comes with a how-to manual to take you from where you are today to that finished goal.

If someone would just point the way, you'd charge ahead. But instead, you settle for another ordinary day. You do the same-old, same-old and cross your fingers that the answer will land in your lap one day soon. Until then, you're resigned to just feel stuck.

Regardless how you landed here or which of these things are holding you back, we can all agree on one thing—it sucks to feel stuck.

But here's a piece of good news: you're definitely not alone. Everyone has been there. And you know what's even better news? You don't ever have to be there again. Because in the same way that your brain leads you into this mess of being stuck, you can use the exact same methods to get unstuck.

As natural as it is for you to fall into this loop where every day feels like you've stepped into a pool of quicksand, there's an equally natural way to instead step directly into action. Instead of getting stuck, you could move directly from that restless energy to doing the thing that would make your life better. And the best part of all? It's a lot easier than you think.

Successful People Feel Stuck

By now you're wondering how in the world we went from my accidental cake to this deep dive into the origin of stuck. You'd much rather just turn the page to find a quick checklist that solves it all, a recipe for success. But here's why fully understanding the stuck feeling's arrival will help you to solve the problem.

It's because every single person who had an idea and went for it also felt the sneak attack or the lightning strike of life's changes. We have to look closer at them to understand why they took action and didn't just stay stuck.

Even Manjhi fits the mold. Before he carved through the mountain, he had been stuck on one side of it for his entire life. He'd been an adult, capable of picking up a hammer and chisel for decades. So, we can say that for many years he fit into the sneak attack definition of stuck. Wishing things would get better, hoping for a government decision to blast a road, maybe chatting over dinner about getting all the villagers together to work on this project. But then year after year, they woke up to the same unchanging mountain. No one took action.

Manjhi also falls into the lightning strike category. After all these years of being cut off from the world and the inconveniences that mountain caused him and everyone around him, tragedy struck. One scorching hot afternoon, Manjhi's very pregnant wife, Falguni, set out for the farm where he worked. She would have to climb an extremely dangerous path on the mountain to reach him with a bundle of food and water for his dinner. Before she was in sight of the farm, she slipped and fell. She was injured so badly that no one in the village could help her. If Falguni couldn't reach a doctor, she and their baby would die.

Remember though, it was a fifty-mile difficult walk to the hospital. Manjhi sent for a doctor. It was night by the time that doctor set out for the remote village, so the steep mountain where Falguni had fallen was too risky. He had to instead take the fifty-mile trip around that mountain. Manjhi and his friends did everything they could to keep his wife alive until the doctor reached them. It felt impossible, but Manjhi's fear and grief pushed them all to keep trying.

By the time the doctor arrived, worried and exhausted, they had little hope that Falguni or her baby would survive. So, when the doctor was able to deliver a healthy baby girl, the villagers hugged and celebrated. They sighed with relief over the good luck that had finally come their way after so many years of every good thing feeling just out of reach. But that's when the worst thing they could imagine happened right in front of them, and there was nothing they could do to stop it.

Falguni died. There was nothing the doctor could do.

The long wait had been too long. The delay of that long mountain pass was fatal.

Manjhi walked through his village, now a single father with a son and a newborn daughter. The weight of his wife's tragic death and the wall of the mountain that had caused it made him feel more stuck than ever.

And by now, you recognize this familiar pattern. You feel it right along with Manjhi. But here's where Manjhi's story takes the turn you've been waiting for, because unlike all the times before when he'd felt stuck, and unlike all the times you and I have felt stuck, this particular time, Manjhi had the confidence to leap into action.

I know the reasons that this particular time felt different for him may seem mysterious, but they aren't. In fact, they follow the same pattern that thousands of action takers throughout history followed. And this is the best part: the thing that moved all of these people forward follows the exact same pattern as the thing that got me up and moving to bake that cake.

And the same thing that got me moving to build that house.

Success Follows a Pattern

Picture Manjhi on a cold dusty morning at sunrise, walking confidently up to the mountain and declaring that it could no longer stand in his way. His children wouldn't face the same barriers he and his wife Falguni had faced. They would have a clear path forward. Manjhi saw it. He believed it. Then with the purest focus and determination, he sold the family's three goats to buy a hammer and chisel. Then he picked up a chisel and made the first strike.

That, my friend, is exactly the level of powerful determination you're going to bring to your next goal.

But wait, why in the world would you listen to me on this? With all the magic pill solutions out there for solving procrastination, all the quick tricks to get unstuck, what makes me the right person to share something completely unconventional?

Because I've been so stuck that I wasn't sure I'd ever get moving again. I remember waking up day after day as a single mom with four kids and just trudging through what felt like the same old day again, and again, and again.

I knew I could have a much better life. I was capable of so much more. What was I waiting for? It wasn't ideas. I had a pile of big ideas. But remember—because I couldn't or shouldn't—I wouldn't. That's what I had always told myself. I waited for things to calm down. And I told myself that it was smart and responsible to wait for these things. The right moment would arrive. I would know when the time was right. But, of course, the time never felt right, and there were always more reasons to wait. So, no surprise, I never took the first step and those ideas floated endlessly on my list as my someday projects.

I was exhausted. I'd survived really terrible domestic violence and being stalked for more than a decade. My finances were in ruin. I worked hard every day but in the narrow, same-old, same-old kinda way that felt like treading water. I wanted life to get massively better for me and my kids, but working a little harder for longer hours doing the same thing wasn't going to add up to massive changes.

The math was clear. Doing the same old small things will never suddenly and spontaneously add up to something big and new. I knew that was true. I knew I needed to do something different. But I didn't know which things to change. I didn't know where to begin.

This may sound familiar to you. I had this feeling, this restless kind of feeling, that I was capable of doing a lot more than I was doing. That my kids and I were capable of building a life better than the life we had. Most likely, you've been there, too. Stuck in place but knowing with every cell that you could be and should be somewhere better.

I knew that people with less than me had accomplished more. And that meant if I could just somehow find the right system, it was possible for me too.

So as a senior software architect, I put my analytical mind to work. I turned to the internet and tried a handful of goal-setting systems. I made flowcharts and charted my progress in spread sheets. I read more than a dozen books. And the ideas I found felt good for a while. They got me busy filling out workbooks and calendars and getting even more organized. I focused on the baby steps. I muttered positive things to myself, and I put post-it notes on my mirror. But one after the other, any progress from those methods just fizzled out. I fell back into the same stuck feeling. The same procrastination habits, and the same-old, same-old small everyday things that weren't going to get me anywhere big.

Until one day I started paying more attention to what *did* get me moving. And I took notes about the things that kept me moving even when a project was hard. You know what I discovered?

I saw a familiar pattern. It was a simple pattern that didn't start with me.

I began looking more closely at people like Manjhi and his mountain. And I found Julia Child learning to cook at 36 and then building an empire of a business. I discovered a postman in France who began picking up pebbles on his mail route and used them to build an actual palace. I read about one of the most amazing gymnasts of all times, Simone Biles who became a champion against all odds. And do you know what I saw in the details of each one of these people hitting massive goals?

I saw the same pattern.

I saw them walking the same paths to success again, and again, and again.

A Single Action is All it Takes

That's why on a cool fall morning when my kids and I were months away from losing our house, I decided to make an unconventional move. I knew that if Manjhi could move the mountain, if Sir Roger Bannister could run a mile in less than four minutes, and if Louisa May Alcott could publish Little Women in 1868, even though everyone told these people it was impossible, then I could do something impossible too. I could do something outrageously big.

In fact, one of the most important things I learned from all these people was that setting an outrageously big, impossible goal was one of the deciding factors to their success.

As luck would have it, I was ready for something big. The

big thing my kids and I needed most? That was easy. We needed a place to live. And if big and uncommon was the path to success, if stepping outside my normal patterns and being unconventional was the answer, then I was prepared to go all in. What I did next was big, but because I was following the formula it didn't feel big at all. It felt natural. It felt like the most obvious solution and like a sure success—because it was.

On a cool fall morning that was for all intents and purposes no different than any other, I got up and had a great idea that would change things for the better. And on that day, I did something radically different. I immediately took the first step.

I declared that my kids and I would build our own house. Really build it from the ground up with our own hands. We needed a house, and we would build one.

No, we didn't know how to build a house and we didn't look like the sort of people who would tackle this sort of a project. Not even close. I was a 110-pound office worker. Sure, I was an architect of sorts, but the ones and zeros of software development are a far cry from two-by-fours and roof rafters. My kids were small and weak. (The youngest was only two.) I had no experience building houses or anything larger than the bookshelf that I had made from scratch the year before.

But I had the help of a brand-new website called YouTube. A site that would not only teach me how to set a concrete block, it would also re-train my brain to reach for goals in the most efficient way.

Tools weren't completely new to me either. I had used

lots of them for small projects, so I knew the basics. I knew how to pound in a nail and I knew how to cut a board. If I did that over and over, I'd end up with a house. Right?

Well, as it turned out, yes, that was exactly right.

These basic skills were important, but they weren't the most important thing I had on my side.

Most importantly, I now knew some of the tricks for setting up a project in a way that made it easy to get myself up and moving, and easy to keep moving. I put those tricks to use on day one, and as I worked, I learned how to apply the computer tricks used in the tutorial videos to make the best use of my stubborn brain.

It all comes down to this: I took the first step, got myself unstuck, and it was mind-blowingly simple.

Wait. Hold on. That's not entirely true.

The physical work wasn't simple—not even close. No, building a house was brutally difficult and exhausting. What I mean though is that setting things up so I could get up and moving—getting that project rolling down the right path—and then continuing forward until I had completed an entire house, that process felt natural and easy.

And to be clear, when I say my kids and I built a house. What I mean is that we set the foundation blocks, framed windows and walls, and ran all the plumbing and gas lines, even made our own countertops out of concrete. We built an entire house. Not a small one either, in nine months we built a five-bedroom, 3,500 square foot house with a three-car garage, a huge shop, and a two-story tree house. Through that entire process, we were also working on a more important project, we were re-building our family.

While healing from years of trauma, our time together building the house helped us create a solid foundation for how to interact as a healthy family. We grew stronger, closer, and smarter. And there's more.

After we moved into the house that we built with our own hands, we practiced applying what we learned to another goal. And then another one. We haven't stopped setting and reaching big goals yet.

Because, remember, these same patterns work for everyone and for every type of goal. When you learn to understand and use the most basic and strongest pathways in your brain to your advantage, big goals and big success will become your constant companions.

You can be like me and like Manjhi, whether you want to build a mountain or tear one down.

Now It's Your Turn

As we take a closer look at Manjhi and his mountain, one of the most important things we'll uncover is: Why.

Why did Manjhi make a move on that particular day at that particular moment? It wasn't the first day of the problem. It wasn't his first day in the village. Why didn't he start twenty years earlier or later? What circumstance created the inciting event—that first hammer strike? How did this man light a fire under himself at this moment that was so big it was impossible for him to resist or ignore?

Essentially, we're asking this: *How do I make today the day I take the first step?*

Because if we can answer that question, reason says we

can replicate it. You can light a fire that pushes you with the same level of determination toward your mountain.

Remember, the day I started wasn't the first time in my life that I needed a house. How did I move from the mere idea of having a new house to actually leaping in to make one?

The same way I landed in my kitchen baking a lemon Bundt cake on an ordinary Tuesday that had no reason at all for a cake.

From the first day of my house project, I was all in with full focus and determination. And like Manjhi, nothing—no amount of ridicule, bad weather, bruises, debt, setbacks, or ANYTHING—could have stopped me. Once I crossed that action line, there was no going back.

If you're thinking this makes me some kind of natural born doer, some non-procrastinator, some anomaly who has never played a time-wasting game on my phone, think again. I've put off calls, ignored emails, and skipped fixing the leaking shower for a weekend Netflix binge. I've gone on a random spring-cleaning binge two hours before a writing deadline just as often as the next person. And you know I've baked a cake when I should have been doing literally anything else. But then I figured out how to stop procrastinating. Not just for the little goals, but for the big ones too. Especially for the big ones. And that got me thinking.

I know how to be the sort of person who picks up a hammer. I know how to start typing and keep going until I have an entire book. And then start another. I understand how some of the most extraordinary people have taken the first step toward their big goals. If I outline exactly what moves me across that procrastination line, then I could help push you and a whole pile of people around the world to get up today and take the first step.

One man carved a path 360 feet long, 30 feet wide, and 25 feet deep through a ridge that was over a billion years old. One mom built a house with her kids by watching YouTube videos. If this doesn't motivate you to tackle your next goal, I don't know what will.

This book is about taking action. About not just identifying the mountain in your life that needs to be moved, but about picking up your tools and moving it.

Now the choice is yours, and nothing could be more important.

Are you ready to take the first step?

CHAPTER TWO

Fight, Flight, or Freeze

BELIEVE YOU CAN AND YOU'RE HALFWAY THERE.
- THEODORE ROOSEVELT

My kids and I used to have a full-sized gorilla costume. And, as surprising as it may sound, owning a thing like that isn't all fun and games. I actually learned an important thing or two from that costume. First, I learned that there are two types of people in the world—the people who would carefully pack a gorilla costume in a trunk and find maybe two reasons to wear it in their entire lifetime, and people like my family, who gleefully pulled that smelly rubber and fur head around their shoulders so many times that the whole costume went threadbare.

That's right, we wore out that gorilla costume.

Most of the time, the kids used the massive fur ball to play zoo or to chase each other through the house on a rainy day. Since it was an adult-sized costume, they looked a lot more ridiculous than terrifying with the massive head rocking on their shoulders like a bobble head and the arms and legs dragging along behind. Even our dog—after the first few panic attacks—just sighed when a gorilla ran down the hall. But on one exceptionally cold Halloween night, that gorilla took a terrifying turn.

It was the first Halloween where the age gap between my kids created a family conflict. My oldest two wanted to stay home and pass out candy to trick-or-treaters, but the youngest still wanted to go door-to-door. We compromised with a time split. The big kids would hand out candy while I got the youngest fully costumed, and then we'd all go out together.

The big kids made the most of their time by preparing a week in advance with faux cobwebs in the windows and scary music blasting on the porch. And exactly like you expected, the pride and joy of their scheme was our full-sized gorilla costume.

I had watched them planning all week, positioning the gorilla on a folding chair under our dim porch light, arguing over the location and whether or not he needed a footstool. They planned to put a huge bowl of Dum Dum lollipops on the gorilla's lap and tape a note on his chest that said simply, "Take one."

You get the idea. It looked like a pretty straight forward plan. A casual vibe of: *Sure, we're odd, but nothing to fear here. Just grab your candy and move along, please.*

But as you might have guessed (even though I hadn't yet) there was definitely something to fear.

On Halloween night, after I went inside to help my youngest with a complicated face paint plan, my oldest son Drew climbed into that gorilla costume. How did I not see this coming?

Well, you know me well enough by now to know that I'm ridiculously optimistic in all areas of life, including the scary things my kids might get up to. What happened next should have cured me of optimism forever, but of course you know it didn't.

Once Drew was fully furred out in the costume, he slumped into the chair with his eyes closed and limbs limp. He sat perfectly frozen when the first little kid walked up for candy. The same for the second and third. But suddenly and with no warning, when the fourth little guy reached into the bowl, the gorilla sat straight up, eyes wide, and let out four gentle gorilla grunts.

That's it. No leaping up, no gorilla-gloved hands snatching at the kids' wrists, they didn't run kids down to steal their Reese's cups. The gorilla only made the slightest come-to-life movements followed by those barely-there grunts.

Which is apparently exactly the right combination to launch a very effective reign of terror.

From inside the house, I didn't think much about the first couple of blood curdling screams from the porch. It was Halloween, and a few screams were all in good fun. Right?

Besides, it wasn't all screams. There was laughter, too.

At least a dozen small trick-or-treaters had been traumatized by the time I opened the front door just in time to see a linebacker-sized dad frozen in wide-eyed terror in front of our gorilla. I blinked. The gorilla blinked. And just like that the dad was gone, running full force down the street, huffing in time to his footfalls.

I know what you're thinking, it isn't all that surprising that someone ran like crazy from a massive scary animal, is it? I mean, who wouldn't? That smart survival move isn't the least bit shocking. But one detail about his dash across town might astonish you.

That dad left his four-year-old daughter behind. Just left her standing all alone in the most adorable ladybug costume I'd ever seen.

She stood at the edge of our porch, maybe a foot from the gorilla's knees. She was just as wide-eyed and terrified as her dad had been, and just as frozen. Her little ladybug wings fluttered when a gust of icy wind blew by, but other than that she was statue-still.

By the time her dad cleared the next block, I was at her side with a fistful of lollipops. The candy didn't matter to her one bit. She didn't seem to hear me or see me. Her gaze was locked on that fur and rubber mask, her feet were locked in place. Her eyes bulged wide, and she was breathing so fast that her little nostrils flared like a race horse's.

My kids, realizing they'd gone too far, started back pedaling. They turned off the scary jungle music and said sweet things to the little girl, dangling lollipops in front of her face the whole while.

The gorilla took off his hands and then his head, turning

back into my son. Our whole family cooed and talked and joked with her. We complimented her polka-dotted face paint and offered her chocolate. But none of this mattered. She remained stock still and silent.

It felt like forever before her dad came dragging back up the street and then slowly up our driveway. He was embarrassed. He had no idea why he had reacted so strongly, and he was horrified that he'd run off and left his kid. He was in a hurry to collect her and move on to a kinder, gentler home on our block.

You probably have some idea what happened to that man. Terror set off his primitive fight, flight, or freeze response. (Because each of these three reactions to terror starts with the letter F, this response is commonly called the F3 response. And that's what we'll call it too. Fight, flight, freeze = F3.) This automatic F3 process happens in the deepest part of our brains. We can't control it, and it's split-second fast.

This response is one of the major reasons humans survived on the planet in primitive times. We have a very effective, built-in response to save ourselves when something dangerous appears out of nowhere.

Here's how it works.

The instant something really terrifies us, we freeze. That pause gives us time to select the best action. Maybe you've seen a mouse do this when he ran around a corner and landed nose-to-nose with a cat. He seemed paralyzed for a split second while he evaluated and eventually chose a fight or flight action—either leap at the cat and bite his nose or run like mad back to the mouse hole. These reactions help prey survive a lot more effectively than a blind panic that could send them into a worse situation. Here's what's interesting about this.

No past experience is needed for this to work. That little girl and her dad had probably never run into a gorilla before. No one taught them to freeze or to run when this happened. There were no gorilla rehearsals. This father and daughter were not connecting an actual experience to their reactions. They were pulling from the experience of past generations—experience that's now actually hard-wired into our brain at birth in order to instantly, automatically react to danger.

This instinctual reaction is universal for every human everywhere. It's pre-packed in our brains.

I know what you're thinking. Shouldn't part of this instinct include protecting your child, too? And the answer is: not always.

When something triggers this response in an extreme way, that deep part of your brain has one objective and one objective only, to keep you alive. You're launched into action with no time to evaluate if you're responsible for anyone else. That means the dad's response worked exactly as it was designed. He didn't do anything wrong. He would 100 percent survive an encounter with a big scary beast. His actions were perfect—at least from a purely biological and survival standpoint.

That makes the dad's response the least interesting part of this story.

Feeling Stuck is a Primitive Response

Let's talk about that little ladybug of a girl though. Because her reaction was as ineffective as it gets. Her level of deer-in-the-headlights paralysis in the face of danger is not good. But it's such a common reaction that we can all empathize. I mean how else would we all instantly understand the phrase: *deer-in-the-headlights?* We know what a deer looks like when fear paralyzes him like this and we know without a doubt that things are not going to go well for that deer.

In fact, that level of frozen fear paralysis just about guarantees you're going to get run over or eaten by something with sharper teeth and a bigger stomach. But if this extreme level of paralysis is such a bad survival instinct, why does it happen so often?

Why did the little girl freeze up and stand right in front of the scariest thing she had ever seen—the very thing that sent her dad running down the street like a madman?

For the answer, let's look at the dad's perfect reaction. He also froze. But it was a split-second freeze, only long enough to process which of the F3 responses would be the most likely to keep him alive. And he acted the instant he saw a way out—in this case that was a clear path down the block.

This proves that pausing is an important response. Sometimes, on very rare occasions, it's a good strategy for a longer period of time. We've all seen this too. It's where the phrases "playing dead" or "playing possum" come from. But to be clear, playing dead is rarely your best survival strategy. For humans in particular, the freeze instinct should be more of a pause instinct. Because when we're scared, taking instant action without thought is what we call panic. And panic is never helpful. Panic could send you straight into traffic, or into a whole pack of Halloween gorillas instead of away from them.

We can all agree on one thing right now. Pausing is good.

Unless of course, you pause for too long.

You know what pausing too long feels like? That little girl felt it. She felt restless and antsy. Adrenaline was running through her veins. Her heart was beating fast. She was taking quick, shallow breaths, flooding her system with oxygen. She felt like she could and should do something, but she just didn't know how to take the first step. Pausing too long made her uncomfortable in her own skin. It made her want something different to happen. But with no idea how to make it happen, she was paralyzed. She felt like (drumroll please) she was stuck.

Sound familiar?

It should. And it's not a coincidence. The thing that stuck that little ladybug girl's feet to the ground is the exact same thing that stuck *you* in place when you should be moving forward. That's right, the same brain pathways that froze her are freezing you.

Yes, red alert. The call is coming from inside the house! The thing holding you back, is your very own brain.

This. Is. Huge.

Feeling stuck is the perfectly normal freeze reaction that's part of your F3 response. You're *supposed* to have these pause moments in life. And they are supposed to happen when you need to leave the spot you're currently in. Exactly like that dad's brain knew that even a linebacker-sized dad was not supposed to stand still in front of a gorilla.

Whether we're talking about the sneak attack sort of stuck or the lightning strike kind, something in your life triggered your freeze response. That freeze response left you feeling stuck. And instead of it being the briefest of split-second moments, you were stranded in an in-between limbo space for far too long.

Remember, feeling stuck is not the problem, staying stuck is.

Use your F3 Response

Before you search your memories for gorilla-sized terrors, let me warn you that in our modern world gorillas aren't usually the problem. The problem is that your brain got so good at striking this alarm at the first sign of fear, that the alarm now sounds off for fears that look a lot more like minor decisions than like chest-beating gorillas.

That's right, your brain can send you into a freeze response for months over things that should barely be a hiccup in your day.

For example, let's say you're unhappy in your current job. The most logical action is to get a different job. But your brain follows that story down a dozen pathways to a dozen different outcomes—all of them creating a wiggle of anxiety over the what-if scenarios.

What if the next job is too hard?
What if you fail?

What if your boss is a psychopath?
What if you hate that job?
What if you fall off a cliff driving to that new job?
What if your family/friends/coworkers alienate you or ridicule you for leaving the current job?

It doesn't matter how unlikely any of these things are. Each wiggle of fear sets off your F3 response. And you know what that means.

You freeze. Right there in that old unhappy job, you take a pause that's only meant to be a split-second reaction before you leap forward and you instead stretch it out for months or even years. You can't see an obvious solution because the modern problems and solutions don't fit neatly into the primitive wiring in your brain. Neither fight nor flight look like the right move. You can't simply fight the current boss for making your job lousy and sprinting out the door definitely isn't the solution.

A solution does exist—you know that. But you don't know exactly what steps to take or in what order. So, there you are. Antsy. Restless. Uncomfortable where you are, but feeling that awful resistance to the first step.

You stand as still as our little ladybug girl facing off with the giant gorilla.

The same pathways keep you in the same unhappy job year after year, or on your sofa with Netflix instead of painting your dining room, or just plain doing the same-old, same-old when you want something so much better.

Thankfully, there's an easy solution that will get you up and moving as quickly as that dad sprinting down the street. I told you that gorilla costume wasn't all fun and games. I really did learn some important stuff from that furball.

The reason the gorilla story is so important is because it demonstrates that survival—or a more important word for our purposes, *success*—happens when we move quickly through the pause and into action. There are a lot of reasons this is true, and we're going to get to them, but I want to point out one of the most important reasons now while the gorilla story is fresh.

Imagine how much energy and power propelled that dad's sprint down the street. His mind and body sent him a tremendous surge of energy so he could take action. He didn't have to call up that energy or think about it. As soon as his F3 response engaged, the burst of strength rushed through him. And there was nothing special about this particular man.

The same little gift of a response happens to all of us. Even the little girl who was standing still, not moving a muscle.

How can that be true?

Well, you've felt it. A restless energy, an antsy feeling that you have to DO SOMETHING shoots through you. And if you don't act, it leaves you feeling pretty miserable. Like a windup doll ready to spring, but your gears are all jammed up. This is what's behind every uncomfortable thing you feel when you feel stuck. It's the result of the unspent energy your brain and body delivered the second they detected the need for change.

And this right here is why it's so incredibly important for you to move quickly through the pause and into action. When you move fast, you harness that surge of flight energy and instead use it to launch yourself directly toward your goal. Imagine what it would look like if your spring-loaded potential were put instantly to use. You'd be miles and miles ahead and it wouldn't feel like it took much effort to get there.

What this means is that you can take the very thing that was sending you in the wrong direction, and use it to take you exactly where you want to go. You can use the way your brain already works to actually reach your goals.

And this works for every person every time. Because remember, we all have the exact same built in, automated responses. This innate, reflexive action that has been holding you back can be used instead to propel you forward.

Push the Play Button

If this sounds new and mysterious and slightly impossible to you, now is the time to relax. Because you've actually done all of this before.

You did it when a how-to video popped up on your screen and you suddenly did something you never planned to do. You dove in quickly and did a thing you never would have believed you could do if that video hadn't given you the confidence. One second you were clicking play, and the next thing you know you've accidentally baked a lemon cake, or built a house.

Even if you've never followed a video tutorial in your life—Dashrath Manjhi certainly hadn't—you've experienced this accelerated, perfectly structured pull into something you didn't plan to do. Here's another example that has happened to every one of us.

You're settled in for a quiet Saturday at home. It's been a long week and the last thing you want to do is, well, anything at all—especially if other humans are involved. But then a friend calls or knocks on your door and announces that the two of you are going for lunch, or to a boat show, or car lot, or maybe it's a candy warehouse or a hang-gliding adventure. It really doesn't matter what that thing is, but it was absolutely not on your to-do list for the day. Not even remotely. Yet somehow your friend had you on board and out the door in seconds.

How in the world did they do that?

Before you knew what hit you, you went from not-gonna-do-it to having the time of your life. In a split second you were up and accidentally trying something new, or going someplace unexpected. And even though it all started far outside of your plans, you wouldn't change a thing.

How does this happen? How do these tutorials or these friends move us to action when our own ideas sit stalled on idle for weeks, months, or years? And most importantly, do these videos and these friends have anything at all in common?

I'm so glad you asked.

Because yes, the sneaky tutorial videos that have you firing up an arc welder in your garage at two in the morning (wait, is that just me?) and the sneaky friends that keep you out until two in the morning both use the same techniques to get you up and moving. But that's not even the exciting part.

The exciting part is that you can easily replicate these

techniques to create a system that gets you up and moving quickly on any idea that pops into your head. You can get yourself unstuck. You can step away from the scary gorilla. You can build exactly the career, the relationships, and the life you want.

Stop Fighting Your Own Mind

But if you're like me—and you probably are because like-minded people tend to gravitate toward each other—you're wondering right about now how this system is going to be different from all the others you've tried. Because of course you've tried to get yourself up and moving before. And of course, it didn't work. Not even when you gave it everything you had.

You know beyond any doubt that your goal is possible You've seen other people reach the same types of goals. You read about their success, watch their videos, maybe you even met them. At first, they inspire you. But somewhere along the line you just start to believe that they have something you don't. Worse, you begin to believe you won't ever have what it takes.

You feel alone.

You feel tired, stuck, and tired of feeling stuck.

So, you dive back in and try all the procrastination tips on the internet. You read more books. You follow the "right" people on social media. You know your goal is important and possible. But even after all of this, you still have trouble taking the first step. Why isn't the advice working for you?

Time after time you gather the motivation to finally take

a step. You arm yourself with advice, and time after time you end up stuck again.

First, I want you to understand that your motivation is not the problem. You're not less determined or even less capable. The problem is that you're getting bad advice. Let me tell you what I mean by that.

Most procrastination advice sets you up to fail.

Most methods follow one of two patterns. One category of tips sets you up to battle against the way your mind is wired. Against your perfectly normal behaviors. Against a pathway carved into your brain as deep and certain as the path Dashrath carved through the mountain.

Fighting systems that are a vital part of human nature is a waste of your time and energy. Even if you can push back instinctive reactions for a short time, they're going to creep back in and sabotage your project. And summoning the energy to fight for every goal will spiral you into burnout mode in no time.

These systems may cloud the goal by suggesting you focus on dozens of small goals instead of one big one, until you are lost in the details and end up on the wrong path. Other systems caution you to go slow and make elaborate plans. And while over-planning is bad for a lot of reasons, the worst thing it does is waste the surge of energy that was ready and waiting if only you'd moved quickly.

Your brain is motivated by very specific situations, and it also tunes out and turns off under specific situations. When you attempt to force your mind to jump through the hoops of an action plan with rigid, black-and-white rules, it will suck the fun and creativity out of your soul. When any goal becomes all work and no play, you'll abandon that goal in no time. No matter how amazing a goal sounds at the beginning, it's not worth reaching for if you're miserable every step of the way.

Brain fighting advice isn't the only useless strategy out there.

The other type of bad advice shows up as an overly specific tool that applies only to a specific purpose. Things like: a step-by-step guide to writing a book or how to organize your garage. These tips deliver in a limited what-you-see-is-what-you-get manner. You get a very specific set of tools and checklists that will help you do a single thing. The second your life or your project strays to something that's in any way different from the sample project (and of course it is), everything falls apart.

Even if, by some miracle, these task-specific procrastination tips are spot-on, they will teach you only how to do one very specific thing under exact circumstances. And the bottom line is, without understanding why taking these particular steps in this order will help you succeed, you can't possibly apply them effectively against the next goal, or the one after that.

Think of this like the difference between building a new six-drawer desk from scratch in your garage versus putting together a desk from an IKEA package. When those IKEA instructions tell you to attach piece A to C and then D, you do this even if you have no idea if piece A is the back of a drawer or the side of a shelf. Like a robot you line up each mystery piece and do exactly what you're told to do.

Your desk will look amazing in the end, but you couldn't

possibly take those same instructions and use them to build a boat, or organize your pantry, or start a T-shirt business. Your IKEA desk instructions will get you one desk model and one desk model only every single time you follow them from start to finish. You're not equipped to handle a missing part, lost tool, or any variation along the way.

On the other hand, building the desk from scratch is an entirely different thing. That project will increase not only your carpentry skills, but because you have to fully understand how and why each piece goes where it goes, and also solve some tough problems along the way, you'll be way better equipped to start and finish any project you take on. Your improved skill set goes way beyond the desk.

You could absolutely use your new skills to build a bookcase, and then a boat, a garden shed, or even an entire house. (Go ahead, ask me how I know.)

What I'm doing with this book is taking this idea one step further. Because I know that once you understand the reactions in your brain that cause you to procrastinate, once you really get why that first step is not only exceptionally difficult but also exceptionally important, I know you'll have the tools to start and finish every project of every size for the rest of your life.

That's motivation and success for every goal you ever set. Forever.

A big deal and a tall order, I know.

But we're going to get you there.

Next, we'll look closely at the exact steps used by video tutorials and persistent friends to get us up and moving.

That's right, we are going to dive into the simple psychological strategies behind the press play effect, so we can recreate the effect in our life step-by-step.

Put more simply, we're going to figure out how video tutorials give us a jolt of confidence to overcome our primitive brains.

Or even more simply: How to press your own play button.

This is the moment to toss aside everything you've learned about goal setting. We're going to start from scratch and set up our goals so they're as irresistible as scrolling to the next video on our playlist.

Keep pressing play, you're going to love this.

CHAPTER THREE

The Press Play Effect

I'M GOING TO MAKE YOU SO PROUD.
- NOTE TO SELF

On a cool April night in East Palestine, Ohio, a young man had an idea. It wasn't the first time he had the idea, but it was the first time he pulled up YouTube and found a tutorial to walk him through every step. He told his younger sister about his idea, and even though most people would have told him it was impossible and he should just give it up, his sister supported him right from the start. In fact, she agreed to be at his side every step of the way. She was, after all, as hungry for a cheeseburger as he was.

Minutes after watching a YouTube video about how to drive a car, the eight year old boy—we'll call him Mac—

stood on his tiptoes to reach his dad's keys to the family van. He emptied his piggy bank. And then, very carefully so he wouldn't wake his sleeping parents, Mac loaded his four-year-old sister into the passenger seat. YouTube had shown him how to press the brake as he turned the key in the ignition, how to move the gear shifter, and how to press the accelerator. Eyes on his cheesy prize, he executed every move flawlessly.

After pulling out of the driveway, Mac successfully made a right turn—which was even harder than you'd expect for a small boy because the older model van didn't even have power steering. He proceeded to travel through four intersections, stopping when the light turned red and waiting for it to turn green before he set out again.

In the mile and a half journey from his house to the only McDonalds in the small town—and despite only having a second-grade education—Mac obeyed every traffic law. He didn't hit anything or roll over a single curb, and he even navigated the drive-through window without any problem at all, ordering a cheeseburger, chicken nuggets, and some fries.

When Mac rolled up to the window to pay with the hard-earned allowance from his piggy bank, the overly-pranked drive-through workers weren't even surprised. They just thought, "Here we go again, maybe tomorrow we'll go viral on some YouTuber's prank channel."

Because surely, this kid wasn't driving. His small sister wasn't just casually riding shotgun without her booster seat. Their parents had to be hiding in the back seat of the van. Right? But then Mac slid forward on the seat, stretching to press his small foot on the accelerator so he could pull away with their snacks. And that's the moment the workers realized this was something else altogether.

This small boy really had driven to McDonalds by himself. They knew beyond a shadow of a doubt that something extraordinary must have happened to set all of this in motion. They just weren't sure what in the world that thing was.

But you and I know *exactly* what set off this chain of events. It was the press play effect. Mac was an ambitious young man who had found all the confidence he needed to do something he'd never tried before simply by pressing play on a tutorial video. He hadn't let anything hold him back. Not his sleeping parents, lack of a driver's license, or the fact that he'd never practiced driving a single time in his life was going to slow him down. He had an idea, and he immediately figured out how to make it his reality.

The Irresistible Pull To Action

When the police arrived at MacDonalds and slid into the booth across from the hungry children. Mac told the patrolman simply, "Me and my sister really wanted a cheeseburger."

And so, he got one.

The siblings ate their McDonalds treats with the officer watching over them until their grandparents picked them up. (Their parents would have come, but their van was missing.) And while the police didn't press charges, it's probably safe to assume Mac was grounded for a while, especially from video tutorials. Also, probably from cheeseburgers.

I'm obviously not suggesting for one second that an eight-year-old child should go for a junk food joyride. But stories like this are important proof of how pressing play affects all of us. It works for every person of every age no matter how much or how little experience you have in an industry. And if we're going to plug our goals into this process, we better first understand what it does to us.

The bottom line is: pressing play overcomes your F3 response.

With the press of a button, your stasis is interrupted and you're up and moving. And as you now know, once you better understand how this effect launches you into action, you can borrow the self-starting structure and apply it to every single project you take on.

If you've been hungrily turning the pages waiting for the moment the secret to getting unstuck will just appear and solve everything? This is that moment.

The secret to getting unstuck is learning to press your own play button.

Let's break down how this effect worked for Mac.

To really get a feel for the way Mac went from the video to the driver's seat, you'll have to imagine every step of the video he watched. That's pretty easy since all successful tutorials follow a tried-and-true approach.

Insert deep, dramatic narrator voice, "What follows is a dramatization."

Imagine little Mac (Little Mac / Big Mac, get it? I crack myself up sometimes.) He is sitting crisscross applesauce on the living room floor with a well-loved computer tablet on his lap. He has already mentioned that he's hungry for a McDonald's cheeseburger and little sis says she is too. They both glance wistfully out the window, but McDonalds is too far for walking. The only way to get there is by car. Mom and Dad had a long day at work so they crashed early. And that's when Mac makes the move that changed everything.

He presses that familiar YouTube play icon on a video titled "How to drive a car."

The video opens with a drone-style overhead shot of a smiling young man driving confidently down a scenic street, maybe he waves at more smiling young people and they all wave back. One of them is definitely drinking a can of LaCroix. The car drives off into the horizon.

Pause right there.

Not Mac, he keeps watching this video straight through. But I'm going to pause after each important element to evaluate the press play effect in action. What that means is that this is the *most* important moment, the one you've been waiting for.

Effect 1: Set the Scene

The opening scene of that car driving into the sunset is the key to everything, and I'll come back to it again and again. That's because in order to really buy into a goal, you have to see it. Not in a generic way either, I'm talking about a crystal clear visual of the end result. What I mean by this is that you absolutely must be able to see not only every detail of what your end goal looks like, but also what *you* will feel like when you're living your goal. When a goal is set up the right way, the pull to action is so strong that no one could possibly hold you back from your first action step. Watch how well this works.

Mac wasn't just observing someone else driving a car in that opening scene—it was so much more than that. The visual set the scene so perfectly that he could see *himself* driving that car. He could actually feel what it would be like to cruise down his street to McDonalds for a cheeseburger. And we'll see later that the reason this is so important is directly tied to the way our brains take ownership of things—yes, even pretend things like an imagined drive to get an imagined cheeseburger.

This is really important.

This means that the instant Mac could fully see the results of his goal in his mind—holding that cheeseburger while a drip of warm cheese slid down his thumb—he was already a huge leap closer to actually achieving it.

Setting the scene is always essential, and it's always the first part of any goal. Mac wouldn't have gone to such great lengths to reach his cheeseburger if his only thought had been, "I'm kinda hungry. I'd like to go get some food." A vague goal yields vague action. In fact, a vague goal leaves you feeling stuck.

The more detail you can put into setting up your scene, the better. The bottom line is, you'll never reach a goal that you can't see.

Seeing is more than believing. Seeing leads to success.

Effect 2: Take Blind Action

Cruising right along, let's talk about what happens immediately after a proper set up. Once you have the lights and camera set up just right, next comes the fated ACTION.

This is the thing you're all here for, right? That first action step that gets you unstuck. You want to get up and moving as quickly as possible, to escape the F3 mind paralysis.

After Mac watched that car drive into the sunset, the video cut directly to a single step and the simple instructions to do it. This process didn't give Mac's nerves any time to build up. He had no time to ask himself a few hard questions. He didn't have time to run the idea past someone else. The tone of that video was a no-nonsense message of: you want to take that drive? Then do this.

And with no further drama, the guy in the video said something simple, like, "All you need to do is put your foot on the brake."

And Mac thought, "Well that looks easy. I can definitely do that."

Ok, he probably also zoomed in on this part, his nose right up against the screen while he whispered, "Which one is the brake pedal?"

Then he settled back in, nodding along with the instruction. Can you see what the video did right there?

It began with an important action, but one that was simple enough for anyone to both understand and execute. Even an eight-year-old child with zero experience behind the wheel could do this.

A simple success like this at the beginning of a project changes everything. You instantly feel a confidence boost that carries through your project. And because you've already watched his successful drive, you trust this guy. You feel bold enough to take this blind action—to put your foot on the brake—without feeling like you have to understand the whole process first.

It's mind-blowing how quickly this happened for Mac. Before he even realized it, he was up and taking that first action. He was no longer stuck in a loop of wanting a cheeseburger with no options to get one. That loop was broken.

Mac was unstuck.

Effect 3: Rewind

Primitive mind doesn't only kick in at the very first step of your projects. It's easy to get stuck on other first steps, too. The first step of the day. The first step after lunch. The first step after vacation. Or even the first step of a new phase of your project.

Let's face it, if you pause too long at any point of a project, you'll start to overthink and then quickly freeze in analysis paralysis. That's why Mac's video didn't leave him sitting in the car with his foot on the brake for long. If it had, he would have developed that little tummy flutter that makes you pause any time you step into a project that seems a little out of your league. Instead, that video used a smart and effective trick to eliminate all the nervous responses, including tummy flutter. And this trick is simpler than you'd think.

Because every step can feel like a first step, the trick is to rewind. Wait though, we're not just rewinding to our action step, because if it were that easy, we wouldn't need a book to explain this. If the only trick we needed was just to take action. Then take action again. Then do that again. (eyeroll) Well, none of us would have ever procrastinated or felt stuck in our lives.

Here's what I actually mean by rewind

I mean rewind all the way to the beginning. Mac's video did this. Not literally…but in a summary kind of way. They did this by quickly referencing how they set the scene. They rewound to the goal.

That's right. With just a quick flashback trick, they made sure Mac remembered his goal so clearly that he could still see it and feel it.

Maybe this showed up as a two-second clip of a race car zooming around a track, or even a simple phrase like, "Your open road is only seconds away."

The second Mac completed step one, that small callback reminded Mac why he was sitting in the driveway with his foot on the brake and his hands on the wheel. Just like that he's reminded what it will feel like when the road is zipping away beneath the soles of his size three Keds. He is recommitted to his goal and primed to keep going. As luck would have it, the video is ready to take him the rest of the way.

(In case it isn't obvious, a goal reminder isn't necessary after every single step toward every single goal. You'll learn later to recognize the timing and type of rewind flashback that leads to success.)

What happened immediately following that goal flashback moment in Mac's video? The driver shifted directly into the next action. An action that was at least as simple as pressing on the brake, or maybe even simpler.

"Push the ignition button," they say.

Just like that, the engine vroom-vroom-vroooooooms to life. And with simple actions that anyone can do, Mac feels like he's well on his way to his goal. A goal that would have felt impossible if those actions were presented in any other way.

You've probably already guessed what's next. The video moves directly to the next action. And then the next. Frequently through this entire process, the YouTuber would keep Mac's motivation high by sprinkling in reminders and references to the finished goal. This guaranteed that even when the steps grew more difficult, he didn't lose sight of why the work was worth it. Never, at any point of the process, did Mac stop thinking about his cheeseburger.

A successful video tutorial keeps going through this sequence repeatedly until you take the first bite of your juicy goal. In fact, the best videos keep you moving into each step without any clue or concern about what your future steps might be. You do step 3 without any thought of what step 33 or step 373 might be.

This works because once you're locked in to the visual of your goal so strongly that you can see it and feel it, and once you're moving forward one easily digestible bite at a time, you can't think of a single reason *not* to just keep figuring out each step until you finish the project.

As Easy as 1-2-3

These three steps sound simple because they are: Set up, blind action, and rewind. Here's why these simple steps are so exciting.

We've only touched the very tip of the iceberg here, and already it's obvious that how-to videos uniquely tap into the way our brains are set up to work. That is what I'm determined to do with every part of this book. I want each of us to better understand the way our brains naturally work, and then instead of fighting against it, learn to use the existing system to succeed.

It works like a brain hack. Like a shortcut. Like a fast track to success where reaching for goals feels exactly like it's supposed to feel.

Right from this starting point we can see that instead of fighting against the hard truth that every step can feel like the first step, this structure actually takes advantage of that fact.

And there's so much more where this came from.

The set up and immediate action cycle are the foundation of setting up your own play button. This simple combo is literally the heart of what you need to know in order to press your own play button so you can finish any project or reach any goal.

BUT, WAIT.

Don't run off thinking you own the keys to the kingdom. Because if this goal-action-goal-action-repeat sequence is all you have when you launch into your project, you'll die of boredom (or maybe less dramatically, just quit your project) long before you finish anything.

That's right. No cheeseburger for you.

The real magic behind the press play effect happens the same way all movies create magic, with a touch of Hollywood-style special effects. And it's not until we combine our feature film with these special effects that we're pulled to irresistible action and guaranteed success. The special effects are coming up in the next chapters, so keep space in your head for them while we chat just a little bit more about the three steps.

Despite the fact that foundation work can feel muddy, grueling, and slow, it's the most important part of any project. And I know you have the grit and determination to understand this right from the start. Because once you do, it'll transform every idea and every project you pursue.

That truth hit me like a ton of bricks.

This effect works and the proof of it is realized billions of times a day. Literally, billions. Yes, it's true. This is not one of those one-and-done effects. Around the globe, billions of hours of video tutorials play every single day. In fact, more than half of the videos uploaded to YouTube fall into the how-to category. The effect is the same whether the videos originate on TikTok, Instagram, Facebook, YouTube or countless other social media platforms, blogs, or random websites.

Sometimes we search out a video, and sometimes it pops up when we had no intention of doing anything at all. But in either case, we end up making, baking, and reaching for goals we never imagined ourselves pursuing.

Sure, that first step is a super important one. And of

course we need to get you up and moving on it. But I'm not going to leave you hanging there. I'll be with you until you hit your target. Because when it comes right down to it, every project is a series of first steps. Once we understand how to hack into the cycle set off by the play button, we can set up and reach any goal.

You already have everything it takes to reach bigger goals than you ever imagined. Feeling stuck is about to be a thing of the past. Now that you know the simplicity behind the foolproof method that has moved millions of people to get up and do something, it's time to look at it from a slightly different perspective.

By now you can clearly see how the structure of a video like the one Mac watched can get us up and moving on a project. Even a project you never really intended to do, like my lemon cake, for example.

We have a much larger goal though. We are learning to use this method beyond a video tutorial, which means it's time to take a close look at how people with no access to the internet have used the same method to set up their projects. Believe it or not, the first step into their project was as irresistible as Mac's first move toward his cheeseburger.

You Don't Need a How-To Video

I told you from the beginning that I found evidence of the exact same process used by successful people throughout history. To see what a non-video process looks like, and to get a clearer idea of how we can create this effect on purpose, let's look at some real-life examples of how this method moved people to action long before we were all carrying video players in our pockets.

We don't have to travel way back in time to land in a spot without constant internet access, or even electricity.

In 2001, a seven-year-old boy named John Magiro Wangare started feeling stuck. Day after day he watched his family struggling for hours to do simple tasks because they had no electricity. At night it was too dark for him and his brother to do homework. Magiro's family wasn't suffering alone either, no one in their rural Kenyan village had electricity. And there were no plans for them to ever have it.

The problem was so severe that a family would sacrifice tomorrow for the sake of today, chopping down a tree to burn the wood for a few nights instead of investing in the tree's potential to provide income through tea leaves for years to come.

The only other way villagers could light their homes was with kerosene lanterns. But on the rare occasions they could afford to buy kerosene, they still had to walk almost three miles and could only carry back a small amount at a time. Even then, the pollution from those kerosene lanterns along with burning wood and coal in their small huts created breathing problems. Instead of a solution, the entire village was just sliding deeper and deeper into this disastrous situation.

Nothing changed. It had been this way for decades—centuries even—and no one knew how to make it any better. And you can imagine that to a small boy like Magiro, improving this seemed hopeless.

Needless to say, Magiro knew nothing about electricity

or how to bring it to their village. The nearest electric pole was miles away, so he felt as stuck as everyone else in the village. Until one day he realized he knew a little bit about electricity after all.

On an ordinary day that really was just like all the ones before it, he drew a connection between a basic electricity lesson he'd had at school days before and his brother's small dynamo bicycle light. That light had been around for a while and it wasn't anything special at all. Just a cheap light that couldn't even use a battery. In fact, the only way it could light up was by pedaling the bicycle to spin the wheel. Why was that small light so important?

Because Magiro realized that if spinning a small wheel could create a small amount of electricity, then spinning a large wheel must create a large amount. Immediately, he had a goal. He was going to be the one to bring electricity to his village. He could see that goal so perfectly in his mind. Every small hut would have a light shining after sunset. Electric tools would make life easier and the air safer to breath. People would stop chopping down all of the trees.

Night after night they had all lived in darkness. Year after year no one took the first step to create a power plant. Until, that is, the day that Magiro did. Over the next few years, he found more books at the school about electricity. He learned. He experimented. He located a spot at a river less than a mile away where a waterfall might turn a wheel.

He put a bike wheel in the water, connected it to an old car alternator, and then he stretched a long wire to his house. The water wheel powered a dynamo bike light. Now, he knew for sure that he would reach his goal. He said, "I have a target that in one year, the whole village will light up like a town."

By the time he was 16, Magiro had saved up enough money for a generator. And he was only 21 years old when he placed a large wheel in a nearby river and brought power to his neighbor's homes and even put up street lights. By then he had learned not only how to harness electricity, but also the systems in his own mind that inspired him have an idea and then immediately take the first step.

Today, Magiro Power supplies hundreds of houses with power from the hydroelectric power plant that he built with his own hands. And he's proof that you don't have to have an advanced degree or the highest tech in order to create something amazing. You don't even have to have access to a TikTok tutorial.

All you have to do is set up your project with the same foolproof method to press your own play button.

Creating Your Own Pull To Action

Let's briefly dissect John Magiro Wangare's process to see how it fits our model.

First, the set up.

This one is so clear you can almost imagine the cinematic version of it as an overhead drone shot of this small boy's goal. You see his village at night with a dynamo-style light hanging from the ceiling of every small hut. Power poles connect the houses, with larger lights on each pole lighting the streets and the paths to unify the neighbors and improve their safety. New saplings are growing in the front yards.

Inside, kids are doing their homework, parents are cooking, and everyone is breathing clean air.

The details, the specificity of what this young boy imagined is the very thing that set up his success. Successful people set challenging goals with a high level of detail. Not a vague thought like: *I want things to be better.* Or even, *I want electricity.* But a crystal-clear vision of the end goal that feels so real you could walk right into your vision.

I'll get into why our brains need this in the next chapter. For now, knowing the origins will make it even easier for you to create this kind of vision for your next project.

Let's look at the effect the detailed set up had on Magiro.

He immediately took action. He didn't freeze under the realization that children weren't well-known for building electrical power plants. He didn't pause when people laughed at him or told him it was too hard. He didn't get all paralyzed when someone reminded him that he was in way over his head.

Without further ado, he dropped a wheel in the water and watched how it spun without anyone pedaling until their little knees ached. Then he tried another thing. And another.

Magiro had an idea, set the scene as a detailed goal, and then he immediately took action. And here's a little icing for that cake. He even used some of the special effects we'll talk about later, too. And it's precisely because of how he set the scene that he was wildly successful.

That isn't that just a wild statement, either. Thousands of studies in goal-setting theory prove that setting the scene is a vital part of success, starting with C.A. Mace's first studies in 1935 and continuing through Edwin Locke in the '60s whose research is still considered the rock of goal-setting. And you want to know the real kicker?

The research studies by Mace, Locke, Plato and countless other philosophers, psychologists, and other smart people all line up perfectly with the strategy behind how-to videos. Here's why that's true.

This effect isn't some new-fangled thing that I made up. It's not something that YouTubers or TikTokers or the internet made up either. It's not a how-to video gimmick. It's a psychological phenomenon that creates an irresistible pull to action when a goal is set up in a particular way— a way that's been perfected in how-to videos.

That's what the press play effect is. It's the irresistible pull to action you feel, so you begin without needing to understand the whole process first.

That's what we're all here for, isn't it. That pull to action. Because ultimately, that's the thing that gets us unstuck.

Whatever you currently feel stuck over is the result of your F3 response accidentally firing against a modern problem that it has mistaken as a threat.

Today is the day you draw a line in the sand and step over it. You leave behind the type of person who was controlled by the old brain wiring and responses you didn't understand. Instead, you become the type of person who charges directly toward the first step of every project no matter how big or how small.

You're ready to take the first step toward a better job, a better relationship, a better house, and a better life. And now you know you're not broken, lazy, or incapable. Your brain is working exactly the way it's supposed to. And now that you understand why your brain reacts this way, you can use the energy of those reactions to launch yourself directly toward your biggest goals.

The modern scary things that you want most in life, the things that would change everything for you, they are within your reach. You know they are possible, and you already have everything it takes to get them.

Now that you know why you started feeling stuck in the first place, and you know the basic building blocks for the foundation of your success, it's time to set up real solutions that you can apply immediately. If a seven-year-old boy was able to structure a goal that catapulted him toward success, I know 100 percent that you can do it too.

CHAPTER FOUR

Set the Scene

A GOAL PROPERLY SET IS HALFWAY REACHED.
- ZIG ZIGLAR

I was not the type of person who would build a house from scratch. Literally not one thing about my career, skillset, or family history added up to me picking up a trowel and hammer to build myself a house. I weighed 110 pounds and could maybe bench the empty bar you're supposed to put weights on. Maybe.

With more failures than wins under my belt, I wasn't exactly the type of person who would (or should) take on a complex project so far out of my league.

I wasn't the type of person to stand out.

I wasn't the type of person to talk a bank into giving me a loan.

I was not the type of person to do this.

I simply was not.

Until I made one very simple move that turned me into *exactly* the type of person to do this.

When the house idea struck like a lightning bolt, I immediately set it up as a goal. And the way I set up that goal dramatically improved my chances of success. And even more importantly, I instantly became the type of person who builds herself a house.

I know this sounds like a radical idea. Some kind of woo-woo, head-in-the-clouds motivational mumbo jumbo. But it's not. It's honest to goodness real live neuroscience in action. Hold it right there, though. Don't let the word neuroscience make you nervous. All we're talking about here is the way our brains work. Specifically, the way our brain stores memories.

In short, humans are kind of bad at remembering things. No arguments there, right?

We're not going to take a deep dive exploration into every detail of how we remember things. But a basic understanding of how our brain manages memories will help us better manage the things that mean the most to us, and also change the way we see ourselves and what we're capable of.

You've already seen that the way I set up my house project is the same way a long-ago YouTuber set up my accidental lemon Bundt cake. The same as Mac's cheeseburger adventure, and John Magiro's hydroelectric power station. Each one of these goals, and your goal, begin with an all-important, crystal clear visual of your end goal.

See It So Clearly You Can Taste It

We already learned that pausing is for the weak, so let's quickly drop a success action right here, right now. I know you're ready for it.

Close your eyes and imagine your end goal right now. Take some time with this until you can see it in such perfect technicolor detail that you feel like you could walk right into your mental picture. See it, own it, feel it, taste it. Go way over the top with the details, even the small ones.

If, for example, your dream is to open a high-end pizza restaurant, then imagine walking up to the door and seeing your name on it. Hear the bell jingle as you open the door. Step inside and smell the dough, the sauce, and the bubbling cheese. Sit at a table and feel the weight of the menu, and then read the name of your signature pizza written in the perfect font. You should be able to see the plate, and the utensils. What color is your table cloth? Can you feel the texture of the linen napkins between your fingers?

Walk through your finished goal in your mind until you know every inch of it.

Even if your goal it isn't a physical thing like a pizza place, you can still do this. Imagine what various aspects of your life will look and feel like after you've reached your goal. What suit or dress will you wear to the celebration party? Who will be across the table at your meetings or at your business lunches? What will your bank balance look like? Your office? Your house?

Go into detail. Really lock it all in.

This isn't just an exercise. It's a legitimate way to increase your success rate based on neuroscience. In fact, you're about 71 percent more likely to reach your goal if you visualize it vividly. And the reason will surprise you.

This technique is a little bit of a brain hack. It's a way to take advantage of a well-known psychological effect called loss aversion. Which is just a fancy way of saying that we humans really hate losing things.

Now, the fact that losing stuff in life hurts is no real surprise. We know and expect that. Lose a $100 bill on a walk? Ouch. Lose an apartment, or an account at work, and that hurts. But what may surprise you is that you have to gain at least double what you lost in order to overcome that feeling of loss.

As you can imagine, your brain works extra hard to make sure you don't lose things. That, simply put, is loss aversion. It's a simple principle based on the way we avoid loss because it feels bad. Obviously, there's a bit more to it, but for our purposes the general idea gives us plenty to work with so we can immediately use this principle to our advantage.

You see, as impressive as your brain is, it doesn't make a distinction between real and visualized experiences. The way your brain understands and stores your imagined walk through your dream pizza restaurant is the same as the way it understands and stores a real-life walk through of your completed dream pizza restaurant.

That's why it's so important for your visualizations to be as lifelike as possible.

Going through this exercise can feel a little weird at first, I know. But it's pure gold after you learn to use this little brain quirk to your advantage.

You'll be in excellent company, too. Because this trick has been used for decades by NASA astronauts, athletes, emergency services, and major corporations around the world. Taking advantage of the way our brain stores visualized events has been an established part of success training for a long time. The reason is simple: because it works.

Here's what this process looks like.

As part of training, an athlete or astronaut will imagine in great detail that they are running the race, hitting the tennis ball, or doing the space walk. They do this regularly, playing entire games or doing complex tasks on the space station from start to finish—all in their own mind. Sometimes they even visualize emergencies and work through contingencies to solve problems.

Now here is where things get really wild.

An MRI scan taken while a tennis player visualizes a serve shows the exact same areas of the brain lighting up that would light when they actually hit the serve on the court. You're already seeing how this could be useful, but it gets even better.

The exact same muscles engage that would on the court. We can trace the impulses from the brain all the way to each individual muscle. The athlete's brain doesn't know the difference. It plays through the same sequence for the imagined serve as it does for the real one. I told you this was wild!

Stick with me here. Because this is where we tie loss aversion directly to visualizing your goal, and that's the really good stuff.

When you visualize your goal as if you've already

achieved it, your brain takes ownership of it. Your brain, on a primitive level, files it away as something you already own. It doesn't matter that the winning serve has yet to be played, or that the restaurant location hasn't been built yet. It doesn't matter that the tablecloths are no more than a fabric swatch on your desk. Your brain doesn't know this.

Your brain just says: MINE.

When you felt that amazing happy rush of walking through your pizza restaurant, greeting smiling patrons, and then taking the first bite of a warm slice of the pizza named after your grandfather, your brain declared boldly: I own this joint.

The more you do this exercise, the more your brain believes you own the restaurant.

The more you imagine that success, the stronger that ownership becomes.

And, voila!

The principle of loss aversion does its thing. Your brain works like crazy to make sure you don't lose the restaurant. And your brain is incredibly efficient. It will work double time to make sure your restaurant stays in your inventory of possessions. And I don't just mean it casually whispers, "Hey, remember that cool pizza place you own?" It's way better than that.

Your brain will automatically run processes and set up situations that will help you get that restaurant.

How does it accomplish this amazing feat?

Well, now that you own the most popular imaginary restaurant in town, every activity you take on, the people you meet, and everything you own will be considered and filtered around your restaurant ownership. Your brain has already adjusted to hold your new restaurant, and without any conscious effort from you it will adjust your thinking and behavior accordingly. I know you're wondering what this sort of a brain takeover might look and feel like, but relax, it's way more cool than scary.

When you happen to be seated next to a chef on an airplane, or when a corner building with great parking goes up for sale, or even when you consider a new car, your brain will simply align those actions with the best way to keep your restaurant. You'll chat with that chef about top-of-the-line ovens and the small details that turn a kitchen staff into an unstoppable team. You'll compare the price of that building sale to your savings account, and you'll even plan your next car around the budget and tasks of a restaurant owner.

You don't have to consciously process any of this. After you lock that visual of your goal deep into your brain, it will automatically shift your actions to avoid losing what it wants to keep.

You'll be alert for funding opportunities, and sources for fresh ingredients. You'll keep the conversation alive at the family dinner table so everyone knows how serious you are about your goal. And this level of dedication is contagious. The more often you paint the picture of what this goal will look like for each of your family members and friends, the more their brains will take ownership of it, too.

And that, my friend, is how you create an unstoppable team not only in your restaurant kitchen, but also in your family and friend group or among your business partners.

Every brain in the room will also want to hold on to your

vividly visualized goals. Because everyone in the room took ownership in some way, and every brain hates loss.

Write Yourself a Check

Here's a real-life example of how actor Jim Carrey hacked into this process, and how perfectly it worked for him.

Carrey grew up poor and his whole family was struggling. But he was determined to pivot their hard luck. Long before he landed any big roles, he was a firm believer in visualizing his goal of becoming a famous actor. So, he immediately went to work owning this goal.

Remember, to take it all the way you have to see it, feel it, own it, taste it.

Late at night he would drive up to the overlook on Mulholland Drive and park in front of a sweeping view of Los Angeles. He'd stretch his arms out and say over and over again "Everybody wants to work with me. I'm a really good actor. I have all kinds of great movie offers."

While he looked over the lights of the city, he would even imagine specific scenarios. There were visualized movie offers from directors he admired, and people he respected telling him they loved his work. He pictured everyone wanting to work with him. Over and over again, Carrey painted a vivid picture of his big goal in his mind.

Then he would drive down from the overlook feeling like a million bucks. Because his brain had taken ownership of those amazing achievements as though he'd really accomplished each one of them. His brain owned the success and wasn't going to let it go without a fight.

Keep in mind at that point, with more failures than wins under his belt, Carrey wasn't the type of person who would get a ten-million-dollar movie deal.

He wasn't the type of person directors called.

He wasn't the type of person famous actors admired.

He was not the type of person to do this.

He simply was not.

Until he made this one very simple move that turned him into exactly the type of person to do this.

At one point in 1992, Carrey doubled down on his goal visualization. He wrote himself a ten million dollar check for "acting services rendered."

He dated that check for three years in the future, Thanksgiving 1995. Then he tucked that check in his wallet where it was a constant reminder of the type of person he now believed he was. Two years later, his father passed away. And because the successful acting career had been their dream together, Jim put that falling-apart check he'd written to himself in his dad's pocket in the casket.

That's how front-and-center this goal was in his mind. It was the thing that defined him to such a powerful degree that it even defined his relationships with his closest family members. Even during his most profound moment of loss and grief, Jim Carrey's goal remained the number one promise to himself and his father.

How did he keep such a strong, laser-sharp focus? Simple. He visualized his end result every day, and his brain did the rest of the work to avoid losing it.

A long year went by after that check was buried with Carrey's dad. And then just before the Thanksgiving of

1995—exactly like he'd dated that check three years earlier—Carrey found out he was going to make ten million dollars for *Dumb and Dumber*.

Moments like these show us that visualization launches us toward our goals. It makes goals feel irresistible. It creates the confidence and even the urgency to take the first step toward that goal. It turns you into the type of person who does that big thing. It does this for people like Jim Carrey, and people like you.

Not because it's magic. Not because I said so.

Visualization works because it activates areas in your brain that your brain then bear hugs. It's that simple. Well, okay, simple may not be the exact term for brain science, but hacking into brain science can be simple indeed.

I know Carrey's method sounds pretty dramatic with the LA overlook, the Hollywood sign, and famous directors and celebrities in the mix. But, seriously, did you expect anything less than high drama from Jim Carrey?

Your own goal set up may come with a lot less pomp and circumstance, but the process is the same, and it still works just as well.

When I built my house for example, the visualization was a lot more straight forward. Celebrities and movie producers were nowhere to be found. Remember, I was still at the early stage of trying to figure out how the strategy behind how-to videos worked. I was basing my entire goal structure for building a house on a random lemon Bundt cake video. There was a whole lot I didn't understand yet. But what I knew for sure is that the way to really get my mind on board, and my kids' minds on board, was to lock that end goal in our minds. So right from the start we focused on the finished house.

Sitting at the dining room table in the house we were about to lose, my kids helped pick out the paint color, the finish flooring, the stain for my library bookcases, and which fabric we'd use for the living room curtains. We drew the plans for the house ourselves and imagined ourselves walking through that house. We even took Roman's little Lego people and walked them around on the blueprint, playing with them like it was a dollhouse.

Long before I knew how to dig a footer or frame a window, I knew what it would feel like to walk in the front door and sit on the sofa eating popcorn with my kids on movie night.

This meant that just like Carrey, Mac, John Magiro, and a million successful people before me, I had an incredibly clear and detailed vision of what my finished goal would look like before I even began. I could run my hands over the curtain fabric swatches and know exactly what it would feel like to stand in my dining room window and open the curtains at sunset. The kids and I used these mental images as bonus motivation through the entire build.

When my 17-year-old daughter Hope took her lunch break, she retreated to the sofa in our living room to eat her fistful of beef jerky. And she did this when the sofa was still on order and even when the living room was nothing more than a muddy patch with a hickory stump in one corner.

Drew did his homework in the library. Even when the library was a concrete floor surrounded by skeletal two-by-six framed walls.

It was the same for 11-year-old Jada when she was knee deep in mud excavating a tree root from our muddy field in the first week of the build and she casually mentioned, "This root is really stuck under the fridge. Not as bad as that one under the kitchen table was though."

We had no fridge and no kitchen table on the construction site. But because these kids had helped design the house and hand draw the plans, and because they had helped pound in the stakes that marked out the corners of the house (and walked Lego people across the blueprint) they knew every inch of that floor plan.

While it would have been just about impossible to make me or my teenagers work brutally hard for long hours in the freezing mud for a house they'd never seen, we had a trick up our sleeves. We had hacked into our brain's tendency toward loss aversion. We could see every inch of our house in our minds, we could feel what it would be like to live there. And once your brain takes ownership of that reality, nothing in the world can stop you from going after it.

We didn't work brutal hours to build some new unseen thing. We worked to keep the house our mind already owned. There is a huge difference in the level of fight you'll put up to keep something you love versus something you just vaguely want but have never actually held in your hands.

This level of visualization set us up for success. It gave us a head start. It made that first action step and every one after that feel irresistible. We worked brutally hard for long hours in freezing mud in order to make owning that house our reality—in order to make it our home.

Everyone can visualize like this. Even if you need a little

practice to really get good at it. So, let's talk about a few ways to begin.

Maybe you're the sort of person who makes vision boards, and maybe you're not. I'm not going to try to arm wrestle you into cutting words and images from magazines to glue to a poster board. But I will tell you that it's a good way to supplement what you see in your head and put a more constant reminder in front of you. If that feels too weird to you, then make a digital goal file with images of everything you want.

"Until it's on Paper, it's Vapor"

All of these things help focus your mind on your target. You have to see the goal to believe it. You have to see it to reach it. But no matter how you handle the physical image side of this, here's one more thing you should absolutely do.

Write down your goal.

That's right, put it down on old fashioned paper with old fashioned ink.

It's one of the easiest success moves you can make. And it's an action that really doesn't get the attention it deserves. Because that simple act of writing your goal down increases your success rate.

It's a well-studied fact that people who write their goals down on paper are at least 50% more likely to achieve them. That's it. Just write it on paper, and *POOF* you've dramatically improved your odds. No special pen or paper needed. Just write down your goal, and you're closer to reaching it.

It sounds like witchcraft, I know. But like so many things that sound like magic, this one is actually neuroscience. And you're going to love the details behind how this works. But first—because I saw you roll your eyes at me—here's some proof.

Bruce Lee, the famous martial artist and movie star, regularly wrote letters to himself, and many of those letters listed his goals. In 1969, when he was 29 years old, Lee wrote a very detailed goal letter to himself declaring that he would "be the first highest paid Oriental [sic] superstar in the United States." By the age of 32, he had done it.

Grant Cardone, best-selling author writes his goals down twice a day, once in the morning and once at night. And Scott Adams, the creator of the Dilbert cartoon took the advice of a friend who told him to write his goal fifteen times a day. He is now one of the most successful cartoonists of our time.

You can find thousands more examples of successful people who attribute writing down their goals as a boost to their success. But how can such a simple process possibly have an effect on your enormous goals? I'm glad you asked.

When you write down a goal, something happens on a neurological level. And it's something a lot bigger than just the visual cue of the lines you've written on your legal pad or the Post It note on your mirror.

Having an external storage place for your goals is a pretty minor benefit of writing them down. Neuropsychologists attribute the value of this process to a much deeper phenomenon called encoding.

If this sounds like the same third grade system you used

for the secret code notes you passed across the classroom to your BFF, then you're well on your way to understanding how this works. Because it's all about the way every thought is deciphered by your brain before the info is stored. Encoding is the process of your brain taking incoming information, and converting it to make it easier to store.

Bear with me here, because I'm about to show you how encoding works with your written goal to help you succeed.

Let's say you write your goal on paper: *I want to run the Boston marathon next year.*

As simple and direct as that sentence structure is, your brain doesn't just store the words. It converts them to lots of things like images, geographical locations, calendars, and even sounds. That means a single goal might hit dozens of parts of your brain through the encoding process before it's stored—a lot like the way your third grade note landed on dozens of classmate's desks before your BFF got it.

Sure, this encoding process happens on some level with every new idea you think of. But certain things can improve the encoding process. For example, there is an identified "generation effect" which basically says that it's easier to remember ideas you generated yourself than ideas you just hear or read.

And when you write down your goal, you get to access the generation effect twice—first when you create the idea in your mind, *I'd like to build a home, own a pizza restaurant, run the Boston Marathon.* And a second time when you write it down, because from that idea you're creating a physical thing that requires you to lift a pen, straighten your paper, think about the scale and spatial relations of each letter, regulate the pressure of your pen, and more.

Writing feels automated but it's not really. You use a lot of cognitive processes when you write something and this creates a double whammy of memory and focus to help you create your goal. Here's where this gets even more interesting.

You have two distinct sides of your brain, the right side and the left side. An imagined goal will stay primarily on the right side of the brain. But writing it down also taps into the left more literal side of your brain, too. And the more you can light up and excite different areas of your brain, the more new ideas your brain will create to surround that goal—and therefore help make it happen.

The signals that start in your brain don't stay in your brain. Remember how the athlete imagining a tennis serve sent nerve impulses all the way to the muscles used in a serve? Your brain communicates with every fiber, cell, and bone in your body. That's how thoughts become actions.

Thinking a goal and then writing it down is a call to action. You're sending a message to every cell in your body that says, "I want this. And I'm going to have it."

As Sir John Hargrave, CEO and author of Mind Hacking, says, "Until it's on paper, it's vapor."

Here's another way to think about this.

The more ways you send an idea through this encoding process, the more space it takes up in your head. And in this case, the elephant in the room gets noticed.

Huge Benefit, Small Effort

Incorporate these visualization and encoding ideas into your daily habits so they become a natural part of what you do. It's not just about believing things in your own mind, saying them out loud and writing them down engage even more areas of your mind and increase your odds of success.

It may seem like these are all different processes happening in your brain, but everything that happens in one part of your brain is directly connected to other parts and to your entire body. No process happens in isolation. You can see how writing things down activates loss aversion reaction in your brain. And also, how visualizing is part of the encoding process. By understanding and using both of these fantastic and automated processes in your brain, you are dramatically increasing your success rate for every goal you set up for the rest of your life.

These methods aren't complicated. They set the scene without taking up much of your time each day. But because they take advantage of the way your mind is already set up to work, you get an enormous benefit for very little effort.

You could take another path. You could sit completely still and do nothing. Because the honest truth is, you don't have to do anything to get results. I'm serious. Don't write a thing down. Don't make a single effort or set a single goal. For the next year, just keep breathing and going through the motions of whatever life sends your way, you will still get results. Guaranteed.

The question is, will they be the results you want?

You already have what it takes to reach your goal. And

now you have the tools to set up the first action so it's irresistible. You're the type of person who launches into your project, and you're the type of person who reaches the goal.

You can do this.

In the words of Roman emperor Marcus Aurelius, "If a thing is humanly possible, consider it within your reach."

CHAPTER FIVE

Action

*THE UNIVERSE LIKES SPEED. DON'T DELAY.
DON'T SECOND GUESS. DON'T DOUBT.
- JOE VITALE*

Since the universe likes speed, I'll get to the point. The solution that finally gets you up and moving is not only easier than you'd expect, it's also something you've already done a bunch of times—especially when following how-to videos. Are you ready?

Take blind action.

That's it.

Take blind action.

The entire concept of how-to videos relies heavily on our willingness to start each step with a blind confidence that all the tasks together will add up to the goal. You jump right in and do one step without any idea how to do future steps. For example, if you're learning how to fold an origami swan, you trust that each step will build on the previous one. You focus on the step in front of you and only that step. You remain blind to all future steps until the one you're doing right now is complete.

This how-to video format is efficient. It works.

Think about what would happen to your origami swan if you do two simple steps then fast forward the video to the complex outside-reverse wing fold in step nineteen. It would be a disaster. You wouldn't know the simple starting folds yet, or have the confidence that completing them would have given you. Even the vocabulary would seem foreign and overly complex. The whole project would feel harder than it's supposed to be. You'd probably feel overwhelmed, and overwhelm leads us straight to procrastination. And more than likely you would abandon that paper swan for good.

If you trust the strategy of that video, you'll reach your goal. You press play, grab a sheet of paper, and make the first fold. It would be simple, and you would feel good about it. Your skills, understanding, and confidence would grow with each fold. With what feels like very little effort, you would complete your first origami swan.

The press play effect pulls you forward exactly like it was meant to.

In your larger, real-world project, it may feel surprising at first that you're allowed to do step one before you can prove that you know how to do step 503. We think this way because we're afraid of being caught off guard. We're afraid of falling flat on any phase, so we over-inflate our need to plan and learn everything before we begin. We research, plan, prepare, and evaluate our goal to pieces.

Our perfectionist level of planning doesn't just slow us down. More often than not, this turns into full out procrastination. We push down the adrenaline-fueled thrill of a new goal until it fades away. We pause long enough that our doubts are larger than our desire for the end goal. We can all remember dozens of times our goal faded away before we took a single action step.

That's why the secret to success is taking a blind action to lock in the goal and build confidence and skill on the job. But just to be clear, this doesn't mean your head is completely in the clouds with zero clues about what overall steps are involved in your project. Of course you have to know the major milestones. Of course you have to secure the supplies, money, tools, and the basic skills. But you don't have to know the details of how to do every single task before you start.

Once you've set the scene and have a sweeping overview of what's involved, dive in and take action on the one step in front of you. You don't have to know how to do the entire thing in order to move one step forward.

Here's how this looked on my construction site.

I bought an empty acre of land within days of having the idea to build a house. That was blind action. I didn't have to know how to build a roof in order to buy the land.

Then the kids and I started clearing a spot on that land to build a house. No one quizzed me to make sure I knew how to set a foundation block before I cleared the land. No one timed me installing a tankless hot water heater before I built walls and windows. Did I know how to install a tankless hot water heater? Absolutely not. But I was completely confident that I could do it when the time came. And that confidence came from two places.

First, I knew I would learn hundreds of new skills between the first shovel of dirt and the day I starting on the plumbing. Little by little I'd learn vocabulary, build muscle, and gain a greater understanding of how everything in a house worked together.

Second, I already had a pile of evidence that I could figure out how to do smaller things like bake a lemon cake, build a bookshelf, or teach myself computer languages. I'd even repaired leaking under-sink pipes before, and replaced both a faucet and a toilet. It's not the same exact process as a hot water heater at all, but they were skills I knew I could expand and apply. So instead of being overwhelmed by the massive size of my house goal, I focused on the smaller skills that I already knew would add up to larger things. Here are some more examples.

My foundation would be made up of 1,500 concrete foundation blocks. I didn't panic and say, *Holy cow, how will I ever learn how to set 1,500 foundation blocks?* Instead, I said, *I only have to learn to set one foundation block, and then do that 1,499 more times.* This slightly different perspective had a huge effect on how possible each task felt for me. I didn't know how to frame a window or a wall. But I did know how to cut one piece of wood and pound in one nail. If I did those two things over and over, one step at a time, I knew I would end up with both a window and a wall.

This meant that when a how-to video set the scene with

a perfectly framed wall, and then began by cutting one piece of wood, I took blind action with confidence and with genuine excitement about the wall I was building.

These are simple examples. But as you've probably already guessed, we're going to follow this strategy to much bigger things. Let's kick this up a notch with a look at how one woman took a blind action step and built a billion-dollar empire.

I knew a story about making bank would get your attention. Let's go.

Take Blind Action

In the early '80s, when Sara Blakely came home from elementary school her attorney father didn't ask about her wins for the week. Instead, week after week he asked her how she had failed. Then he tipped back and waited enthusiastically for her failure story. If she hadn't fallen flat that day, her dad would be disappointed. Pretty soon, she started taking unexpected risks just so she could have a great dinner table failure story to share.

Now, I realize this may sound like a cruel way to mock a kid, but Blakely's dad was actually priming her for success. He was teaching her that whenever an idea struck, she shouldn't hold back for fear of failing. In fact, she should jump right in and take blind action. Sound familiar?

This is how she learned that the kind of failure her dad was asking for was proof that she had tried something new. Something that stretched her ability and therefore her opportunity.

UNSTUCK

Blakely's dad didn't want her to shy away from hard things. By rewarding the times that she struggled, he redefined struggle as a natural part of trying new things. Struggle is part of the process.

The only real way for Blakely to lose in her dad's eyes was if she didn't try at all.

By the time Blakely was 25 years old, she had failed at a lot of things, including becoming an attorney. That's right she had failed the LSAT twice, and she was struggling to find her career path.

She was doing well enough at her interim job of selling fax machines door-to-door that she was named a national sales trainer, but she knew it wasn't the sort of job she wanted to do for the rest of her life.

Thankfully, Blakely had another success trick up her sleeve, and it won't surprise you at all that you've heard of this one, too. Visualizing her goals in extremely specific detail was a constant habit for Blakely. And even better, she wrote down her goals. After a particularly awful day of selling fax machines, she felt a heavy dose of sneak-attack stuck. She pulled out her journal and narrowed her talents to her biggest strength: sales. It was time to play to her strengths.

That day, Blakely wrote her biggest life goal in her journal, and it changed everything. She wrote: *I'm going to invent a product that I can sell to millions of people that will make them feel good.*

She didn't stop there. She also visualized what her ideal, everyday life would look like after she reached this goal. And she did all of this before she had a single clue what she might invent. Having this visualized goal prepared her mind to take a blind action.

Next, she started looking for the big life-changing product she could bring to the world. To absolutely no one's surprise, a big idea didn't just instantly land in her lap. Still, she began every day by restating her goal and envisioning her amazing someday life. Lots of times she was frustrated while she waited for that big idea to strike, but she held firm that it would happen if she continued watching for it. That's when a small wardrobe problem changed her life.

Blakely was invited to a party with some friends, and she wanted to wear a new pair of white pants. The problem was, she didn't feel like she looked her best in them. She liked the way her control top tights from her work uniform firmed her tummy and made the pants less transparent, but she needed a more casual option without stocking seams over her toes.

An idea sparked, and because she wasn't afraid of failure, she charged forward with a blind action. She took a pair of the control top tights she wore in her sales job and cut the feet off. This split-second DIY move didn't just solve her wardrobe problem, it was exactly the sort of invention she'd been looking for. She realized that millions of women would appreciate this solution. In that instant, a firestorm of ideas lit up Blakely's brain.

She had her million-dollar idea, and she was only 27 years old. Can you guess what happened next? Of course you can.

Blakely took another blind action.

She didn't hesitate. She didn't second guess her ability. She didn't pause to verify that she was capable of step 503.

She did the step directly in front of her with full blind confidence.

She moved immediately from setting the scene to taking action.

With only $5,000 of savings, and absolutely no experience in retail, fashion, or running her own business, she wrote her own patent and started a company that everyone—except Blakely—believed would fail. In fact, one attorney thought her idea was so ridiculous that he thought he was being pranked.

This idea was no joke though, and neither was the level of commitment Blakely felt from the moment she cut the legs off those tights and walked into that party. She knew that her company was going to succeed, because she wouldn't quit until it did.

It wasn't an easy or a fast success. She had a lot of failure stories along the way.

Every morning she woke up and visualized her business and personal goals. Then she worked long hours to make it happen. This meant cold calling heads of companies to explain her product idea, and because nearly all of them were men, it went very poorly. They were skeptical of her lack of expertise, and they had no understanding of the problem her product solved. For two straight years every answer she got was a swift and solid "No."

That didn't stop her.

She traveled in person to clothing and hosiery factories throughout North Carolina and found companies to create samples. She experimented with different string and fabric weaves. Before she turned 30, Blakely had her first real prototype. She also had an official patent for her product and a company she called Spanx.

She still had a long way to go, but she had made unprecedented progress toward a huge goal at a very young age. I know what you're thinking about that process.

Whew. She just blindly took one step forward. And then she took another.

And of course she did. Because that's the secret to success.

Ultimately, Blakely marketed and sold her brand-new, one-of-a-kind shapeware product in the same way she had sold fax machines. She pitched her product directly, looking merchants and distributors right in the eye to tell them how her product solved a problem. Yes, she even stood up and modeled her intimate shapewear herself in pitch meetings. She wasn't afraid of looking a little silly. She wasn't afraid of failure. She was all in.

Her persistence paid off when she talked Neiman Marcus into carrying Spanx. But she didn't sit back and relax just because a handful of her products were on the shelves. Her dreams were too big for her to pause. To increase her sales numbers, she did something highly unusual for any department store product. She personally stood in the store hand-selling Spanx to individual customers. As you might have guessed, this relentless persistence worked.

Bloomingdales, Saks, and Bergdorf Goodman soon added Spanx to their inventory.

Plenty of people still thought this entire idea was nuts. Spanx was still a long shot even after all of this hard work. But Blakely continued to visualize her success in extreme detail, including seeing herself on the Oprah Winfrey show. Then one day she mailed a pair of Spanx to Oprah and that's when her imagined talk show appearance became a reality. Appearing on Oprah became the pivot point that skyrocketed the Spanx brand to unprecedented success.

In 2012, when Blakely was only 41 years old, she was on the cover of *Forbes* magazine as the youngest self-made female billionaire in the world. How did she do so much in so little time? What advantage did she have?

She didn't hesitate. She didn't worry about the middle step of her journey until she reached it. That means she wasn't trying to design or fund a marketing campaign before she knew every detail of the perfect string and weave to create her perfect waistband. She did the step directly in front of her. With each hard-won step forward, her skills, understanding, and confidence grew. When she reached that complex step in the middle, she had everything she needed to figure it out.

She set the scene. She took blind action. And she kept doing this again, and again.

In only fourteen years, Sara Blakely turned five thousand dollars into 1.3 billion.

And even though how-to videos weren't her primary teachers, every single method she used followed, to the letter, the same strategy that how-to videos used.

I told you from the get-go that I didn't create this method, and neither did how-to videos. It's the same method the most extraordinarily successful people throughout history have followed to success. How-to videos simply elevate the success rate by presenting the process so clearly that this all-important action step feels irresistible. And most importantly, they present it so clearly that we can easily learn how to replicate the effect.

Starting a new project that moves you toward a top goal is supposed to be exciting. Maybe—dare I say it?—even fun. And it will be now that you're learning to use the same strategies to create an irresistible pull toward your goal. You're pressing your own play button. It's not a complex strategy. But I bet you have a few doubts and fears wiggling at the back of your mind, so let's address those before we go any further.

Pick an Easy Step

Taking a blind action toward any size of goal can be scary enough to trigger your F3 response. But that doesn't have to happen. How-to videos reduce how often your F3 response is engaged by easing you into projects. That's why the first blind action step of every how-to video is something small and easy. Make one fold. Pound one nail. Put one foot on the brake. Paint a single line. Keep it simple.

If a how-to video began with a super hard, challenging first step you'd run the other way. Why would you set up your own goal in a way that sends you running? You can use this same start-simple strategy with your goals.

Your first action step is one of the most important steps toward your goal, and that makes it feel difficult, but it doesn't have to be. Thinking that important steps must be difficult is kind of like saying good things only come in giant packages, when we all know perfectly well that good things also come in small packages. Which brings us to the obvious conclusion that important steps can be easy.

One more time for the people in the balcony.

Important steps can be easy.

In fact, we can expand this to declare that your all-important first action *should* be easy.

The groundbreaking move that will instantly change the way you approach every single big idea for the rest of your life is simple. It's one small adjustment that will get you moving fast. I'm ready. Are you?

Pick an easy step.

That's it.

Pick something easy.

Here's how this works. You're in control of which action you do first. You always were. Your first action can be as simple as a single, small item that you check off your to-do list. A small move that yields huge emotional results. Taking a blind action doesn't sound difficult at all now, does it.

When your action step is simple enough for a third grader, you immediately do it. And just like that your confidence gets a huge boost. This early win signals to your brain that you really are capable after all.

This is more than a gimmick. It's more than a cute little trick to get you moving. Science supports an easy first action in so many ways.

One of the most important is the way we label and perceive the type of person we are. This first action signals to your brain that you're the type of person who starts and finishes things. You are the type of person who gets the degree, runs the marathon, or opens the restaurant. Seeing yourself as the type of person who succeeds is the most valuable perception shift of your life, and it really is this easy to make it happen.

According to our press play strategy, your first action should be a simple step with instructions an eight-year-old could execute.

Remember what happened after Mac's how-to-drive video set the scene with a car driving off into the sunset? The video cut directly to a single action and the simple instructions to do it. In a no-nonsense tone it said something like, "All you need to do is put your foot on the brake."

And Mac thought, "Well that looks easy. I can definitely do that." And he did.

Mac got his cheeseburger. And now it's your turn.

Move Fast

Now let's tackle that big ole hairy gorilla in the room. You are biologically wired to toss up that F3 response any time something feels scary or overwhelming. And that means sometimes, even when you've set everything up perfectly, your F3 response could hit you full force.

But you know me well enough by now to know that we're about to use that fact to our advantage. That's right. You're not at the mercy of that primitive F3 response. Not at all. You can't stop it from happening, but you can stick a steering wheel on it.

The only thing you should do differently when you feel that F3 response hit, is move even faster into your blind action. It sounds counterintuitive, I get it. But it's a strategy that can move you even faster towards your goal. Here's how successful people use it to get ahead.

This survival surge delivers huge advantages that you can use for more than escaping. Moving fast with your F3 response allows you to take advantage of the adrenaline rush it delivers. Instead of sending you running fast and far from your goal, that adrenaline could be harnessed to take you toward your goal.

And because the success of this primitive response relies on speed, the only thing we have to do to use it, is move fast. Sound too good to be true? It's not.

That F3 response isn't only happening in your lungs, muscles, and adrenal glands, it's also making a bunch of things happen in your brain. They happen automatically, and they happen (you guessed it) FAST.

The instant that response fires, your cognitive abilities improve. You can think more clearly, focus more completely, and even see in greater detail. Your brain cells are equipped with extra energy so you can come up with ideas and plans at a faster rate than ever. More than any other time, you can run through scenarios from start to finish and reach exceptionally creative solutions.

In short, your 'what if' game is at its peak.

All of this happens as automatically and instantly as a reflex. A scary new step lands in front of you and *BOOM* just like when the doctor's little rubber hammer hits your knee, your F3 response kicks into action without a single conscious thought from you.

Picture that whole system working to your advantage. That's a much nicer picture, isn't it? Because we can all use every advantage we can get, especially the sort that works on autopilot and makes us better at things. This is how your mind and body were designed to work together.

The best way to make moving fast your natural response will surprise you. Not because it's difficult, but because you've heard it before.

Pick an easy action step.

Yes, the same exact strategy works here. It's a little harder to do this when your F3 response has you wound up, but the more you practice taking an easy step, the more natural it will feel. Creating this habit is worth its weight in gold. Sara Blakely would tell you it's worth billions. This habit makes moving fast with your adrenaline an automatic and easy response. And that takes you exactly where you want to go.

Simon says take one blind step toward your goal.

Magnify Your Impact

See what we just did? We just confirmed that getting unstuck is 100 percent within your control. You can decide to take a blind action by doing one step that takes you closer to your goal. And you get to pick which action you take first. The difficulty level of that action is completely in your hands. You can pick an easy one, and just like that you're unstuck.

Whether you're opening a pizza restaurant or becoming a race car driver, no one can make you do something beyond your skill or comfort for the first action. Even if you're setting a business goal under twelve layers of supervision, *you* get to define the parameters of your first action. This small change in how you view your project launch transforms everything.

Most importantly, understanding how your actions affect your mind in both good and bad ways will help you navigate the tough things and take advantage of the good things. Before I set you loose on the next chapter though, let's take another look at blind action in a real-life project. Seeing how this works, and the motivations and successes of real people does more than just motivate us, it creates a framework for our understanding of each process.

You're going to love how this all comes together in this next example.

Making a billion dollars like Sara Blakely is one good reason to commit to this strategy, but there are other approaches to building big things. Learning how one man's goal can impact the entire world will give you a brand-new appreciation for taking a blind first step.

In 1997, a 44-year-old artist and carpenter from the United Kingdom moved to Cancun, Mexico, hoping to live a simpler life. Richart Sowa had always been the sort of person who cared about protecting nature and creating more sustainable living practices. He was frustrated as he looked for a way to have a greater impact on sustainable living options for the average person. Then one day, an idea struck him.

He was collecting bottles on the beach for cash, and he imagined he could use the bottles to create a floating island. Not just a mass of floating bottles, but a real island covered with soil, sand, and a little house where he would live. He imagined planting mangrove and lemon trees. He'd have bananas, spinach, and tomatoes. He could cook in a solar oven and wash his clothes in a drum powered by the waves. But I know what you're thinking.

Sowa sounds a little bit nuts.

Other people thought he was nuts, too. They watched him fill fishing nets with dozens of plastic bottles, test them on the water, and then do the same with hundreds and then thousands more plastic bottles (approximately 150,000 bottles in total). In six months, he had a floating bottle and net base that was 50 feet across and about 65 feet long. He covered the base in bamboo and plywood. All the while everyone around him told him that this was a terrible idea, and that he was making a mistake. But his vision never wavered.

He didn't worry yet how he would collect fresh water, generate electricity, or make a composting toilet. He had always been a creative thinker, and he'd focus and solve those steps when he reached them. Day after day, he focused on the step directly in front of him, taking one blind step forward after another.

For weeks, Sowa paddled back and forth on a raft with loads of soil and sand until he had created his own private beach. He named the newly born land mass Spiral Island. Then he tackled the challenge of rooting fast-growing mangrove and palm trees so the roots would help strengthen both his bottle foundation and his loose soil top. It took months, but the idea worked.

He planted a full garden and built a house—eventually it would be a two-story house with two bedrooms, three shell showers, a dry composting toilet, and electricity. He also added a cat, some chickens, a duck, and a dog named

Rainbow. Not to mention the ocean life that made homes in the base of his floating island. He learned a lot about using reclaimed materials and educated a lot of visitors. In fact, the Mexican government eventually declared Sowa's island Mexican soil and Sowa made a living welcoming tourists.

Spiral island survived tropical storms and a hurricane, until in 2005 Hurricane Emily broke it apart. As you might have guessed, that's when Sowa began building his next island, which housed him until 2019.

You want to guess where Sowa went after that?

Today he is in eastern Brazil upstream from a resort town called Itacare. And, you guessed it, he's starting his next island. This next bottle-based floating land mass will be heart shaped, and he's naming it Trashier Island. I have no doubt this island will be a success.

In fact, his entire massive idea was a success even as his first island split to pieces in the storm, because building himself an island home was never his main goal. His greater goal was to make an impact on the planet with more sustainable living practices, which he continues to do around the world.

There are a thousand more blind action steps in Richart Sowa's future, and it's safe to say he's ready for them.

Make Action Your Habit

How-to videos deliver such a perfect strategy for getting unstuck that it looks and feels natural as you learn each step. Putting these steps into practice can quickly become a habit that changes your life forever by increasing the odds of your success when you reach for the big goals and the small ones.

There's no doubt that this is a big deal.

Just like it is with how-to videos, your willingness to dive right in and trust the process is essential. You don't have to know how to do the whole thing in order to take one step forward. Say that over and over until it becomes your way of life.

Think of this blind action step as a focus, confidence, and commitment strategy all in one. As little as one completed step works as a public and personal declaration that you're committed to your goal. Because your focus is laser sharp on a single task, you complete it more quickly. This boosts your confidence that you can complete the next step and every one that follows. You can see how powerful this process really is.

And thank goodness it's also incredibly simple.

We have irrefutable scientific proof that each small step forward you make improves not only your odds of reaching the goal you're working toward, but every goal you set for the rest of your life.

Identify one action step you can take toward a goal today, and then take blind action.

BOOM

You're up and running. You're no longer planning to do this thing on a mythical "someday." You are officially off to the races. With one easy step you've become the type of person who reaches for a goal and hits it. This changes everything.

You're not planning to write a book. You're writing a book.

You're not planning to build a restaurant. You're building a restaurant.

You're not researching a podcast. You're a podcast host.

You're not researching a degree. You're enrolled in the class.

You're not thinking about new career. You've started a new career.

You're not thinking about the Boston marathon. You're training for the Boston marathon.

You're exactly where you're supposed to be.

You're unstuck.

CHAPTER SIX

Rewind

LUCK IS WHAT HAPPENS WHEN PREPARATION MEETS OPPORTUNITY. – SENECA

We've spent a lot of time working our way through the earliest moment of project anxiety. That moment when your goal looms large and terrifying and your brain screams one big question: Do I eat it, or does it eat me?

By now, you know for sure that you own the secret recipe to make a feast of this goal. And to make sure your energy stays at a peak level all the way through, let's sprinkle a few more sweet tips over this meal.

Complications happen in every project. We know this, may even expect this, but somehow we're still stunned when *that* particular complication hits us at *that* particular time.

This is why the most frequently used phrase in all of project history is "I didn't see that coming," followed by the universal how-did-I-get-here head scratch.

When things aren't going as quickly or smoothly as that first confident step made you think they would, you may start to question everything. This is when imposter syndrome hits hard, and with each complication you feel more and more like you're in over your head.

What is going on here? How do you keep that early excitement burning even when a small part of you is thinking about turning tail and running fast and far from the 800-pound gorilla in front of you?

First of all, try not to worry. What you're feeling is a natural project hiccup, and you already have the tools to fix this.

I could stretch out the big reveal and drop some hints, but I already gave it away in the chapter name. So, in honor of our commitment to moving fast, let's leap right in.

All you have to do to overcome project doubt is rewind. That's right, just do the same thing we did to get the project moving in the first place.

I'm not just talking about rewinding to our speedy blind-action trick though. To keep momentum high you have to go all the way back to the beginning of your project, that all-important set-the-scene step when you visualize your finished goal with such perfect clarity that you can practically walk directly into your mental picture.

Rewind all the way back to your perfect visualization, and you'll find that your motivation is restored.

Ahhhh. Perfect.

Glad that's done.

But unfortunately, what sounds perfect in theory feels a whole lot different in real life. Because you can't squeeze your eyes shut and imagine the day away every time your massive goal makes your tummy flutter. You probably wouldn't get much done. Also, there are only so many notebook pages you can fill with your goal declaration before your hand cramps and you start having flashbacks to that time in second grade when you got 100 lines for running in the hallway. (Sorry, Mrs. Swanson.)

I know exactly how you feel.

I ran smack into this momentum rollercoaster early in my house building project, and the solution I came up with is now one of my favorite success tricks.

Rewind to Your Why

It was December of 2007, and even in Arkansas where I built my house, that meant the temperature had dipped below freezing. I remember standing in a four-feet-deep trench with ice water seeping through the mud into my old tennis shoes while I sawed through a giant tree root. That sounds miserable enough, but what made it even worse was that it was ten p.m., so it was also pitch dark and I was working by the light of my car headlights.

I was cold, wet, muddy, and starting to panic that if I was struggling this much with the most important and basic part of the house, the foundation, how was I possibly going to do the rest? My brain went into full what-was-I-thinking mode.

How in the world am I going to run the gas lines and build the rafters?

How am I going to run all the plumbing and frame the windows?

What made me think I could do this crazy project in the first place?

Maybe I should just quit while I'm ahead.

Deep breath, scared 2007 Cara. Remember what this is all about.

This next part may surprise you, because my project wasn't actually about what you think it was about.

I bet you think I'm going to say it was all about the house, but I'm not. My goal was so much bigger than a house. As a matter of fact, the house was just one giant step I would make to reach my larger goal.

You see, I never wanted to be a house builder at all, what I really wanted was to be a writer.

The house was a place for my kids and I to feel safe and secure. And it was also a massive project we could take on together to work through some of the tough things we had survived. But my real goal extended way past the moment we moved into our house. It went all the way to the time I would be living and working in that finished house and how I would spend that time. My goal was to spend it writing dozens of books in the library of my new house.

And while you may think the fact that my goals were stacked like nesting dolls is irrelevant, or maybe only mildly interesting, but it's actually the most important part of the story.

Because there is absolutely no way I would have been able to push through the brutally hard work of building a house if the only thing I got out of it was a house. Under no circumstances would I have been able to dive into the mud day after day for some walls and a roof.

What's my point?

My goal, my real goal, wasn't just about what I was building. Instead, it had everything to do with *why* I was building it. The things I imagined in our finished house were deeper than the curtains and paint colors. I saw myself in my library, surrounded by books. And a whole shelf of those books had my name on the cover. A detail like this armed me with fantastic motivation tools.

Now all you have to do is put the *why* behind your goal to good use, and you do that by finding a way to highlight your why so strongly that you're reminded of it constantly, especially through the tough parts. In case there was ever any doubt, you most definitely will hit tough parts.

This really wasn't news to me. I knew I had to keep my eyes on the prize. But you can imagine it was difficult to think about writing books when I was lugging 1,500 concrete foundation blocks across a muddy plot of land. I needed a clear reminder on site.

Writing, "I'm an author" in the mud with a stick fifteen times a day wasn't going to cut it for me.

I needed something substantial. Something that wouldn't wash away in the next rainstorm, and something that would be a sign for me to keep going even when my back hurt and things felt impossibly difficult.

The best possible answer arrived with my dad just after we poured the foundation slab. He got a kick out of the way I'd named my new house. And when I told him about a "someday" project to set that name in stone, he said, "We should definitely do that right now."

So, we set out to make a massive concrete sign. Yes, I said a sign. And I also said massive and concrete. Picture when you drive into a neighborhood and there's a concrete sign announcing which subdivision you just entered and you'll get an idea of what I'm talking about.

My dad started the process by carving letters out of Styrofoam, then we built a form, secured the foam letters, and poured concrete into it. For some reason we did all of this in my garage, which was something like 250 feet from where I wanted to place the sign. But my dad just said, "Bigger rocks than this were moved to build the pyramids and Stonehenge. Quit worrying about it and go get the chain out of my trunk."

Instead of mentioning that hundreds of people had been on site to help move those other big rocks, I got the chain.

Long story short, we used ancient pyramid techniques of rock moving. And it was not easy, but days later, a huge sign declaring my home to be "Inkwell Manor" was propped against a tree near my driveway entry for all the world to see. And it even has a little stylized ink pot and pen after the name.

Inkwell Manor is the name I'd chosen for our house. Clearly this was about a lot more than a name, though. A sign like that is a bold declaration that inside the house I'm building is an even bigger goal, a library that will serve as my inkwell. It would be the place I'd dip my pen to write dozens of books.

Do you see what a massive sign like this did to my brain? First, it activated a loss aversion response, because my brain immediately declared that I own this inkwell and the huge stack of books on that shelf with my name in the author spot. That sign also encoded my goal declaration into my brain, not once as we made the sign, or twice as we rolled it to the street, but every single time I saw that massive sign.

This reminder wasn't temporary. It's still there today. I see it every time I walk the dog. Every time I mow the lawn, or get the mail. Every time a neighbor drives by or a delivery man asks about it. Every time I stand on a stage and someone in the back of the audience sees a photo of my finished house and they wrinkle their brow and ask, "What's that sign about? Why did you name your house Inkwell Manor?" And I say, because I'm an author, and inside of this house, I'm going to keep writing books.

My kids and I don't say, "That chair would look great at our house!" They say, "That would look great at Inkwell." When someone texts, where are you? The answer isn't home, it's Inkwell. And our text group for the family members currently in the house is affectionally known as the Inkwellian group.

Over and over, I'm reminded of my biggest goal. And that's pure gold for maintaining a steady stream of high motivation.

Create Physical Goal Reminders

You can't simply press pause on a goal when it jumps in your face every time you drive up the driveway. It's like taking out a full-page ad every week in the paper declaring your goal. There's also a lot to be said for this kind of a public announcement.

It tells the world that you're accountable. And you're motivated. And more importantly, it reminds you that you're accountable and motivated.

Am I suggesting you mix up some concrete and pour yourself a slab of a sign? Well, kind of. Because if writing your goal on paper sends it through your brain encoding process and makes you 50 percent more likely to reach it, imagine the boost writing it in concrete adds.

Maybe concrete isn't the right medium for your goal. I get it. I don't make a sign like this for every one of my goals either. But I do create a physical representation of many of my goals. I may build a piece of furniture, make a sculpture, paint a painting, or write it on a coffee mug.

I highly recommend making the reminders for your biggest goals BIG. Choose something that takes up physical space in your home or office so you'll literally bump into it every day. Don't tuck your reminder away in a corner, display it front and center.

Maybe you're not much of a DIYer though, and the idea of making something is a whole massive project of its own. I hear you. And all is not lost. You could just purchase the large reminder. But remember, the more areas of your brain this goal hits when it's encoded, the more likely you are to achieve it. So, at the very least, customize it. Go to a website where you can choose the text on your mug, hat, or T-shirt.

Create an artistic reminder that both reflects your personality and the why behind your goal. Select a color, a photo, or a pattern with significant meaning to you. Make it something that speaks to the why of your goal as much as the what. Build a great big elephant in the room—even if you're the only one who can tell it's an elephant.

Bonus points if it's big enough that strangers ask you about it when they see it. Every time you explain what it's all about, you reaffirm your goal and fuel your motivation.

The only restrictions I suggest for this motivational physical reminder of your goal is that you do it AFTER you have at least one step complete so you're well on your way. This reminder shouldn't take up so much time that it turns into a procrastination technique. Quick and easy, create it when you sense you need it, then get back to work.

This physical reminder becomes an automatic rewind button for your goal.

Focus on the Present

As you're struggling over whatever crazy, unexpected thing is in front of you, you may have a tendency to panic over future steps long before you reach them. Kind of like I did when I was standing deep in the muddy trench and thought something along the lines of, *if I can't do this, then how can I possibly do that!*

Danger, Will Robinson.

Once you start careening down this slippery slope, it can be difficult to regain your footing.

I realize you've been taught to plan ahead in great detail, and that it feels like you should gather every single skill and bit of knowledge for each part of your project before you do a single thing. I understand why that level of over-planning sounds like a much safer way to begin a project.

It isn't.

From my long list of reasons why over-planning isn't helpful, let me submit the fact that it hasn't been working for you. You're here because you felt stuck, and that over-planning mindset is one of the biggest reasons that you felt stuck.

As further proof, let's take a look at the way how-to videos present a project to us. Because we already know they successfully navigate us through projects in a remarkably efficient way.

Think back through the tutorials you've watched in your life. Have you ever once seen one that paused in the middle of step seven and flashed forward to a much more difficult step that looked horrifyingly difficult? Has any how-to video in history just suddenly showed what a nightmare was in store for you in step 72 with no context or instruction?

No. Never. Not once.

Because scaring the life out of you is not an effective strategy for any project. It doesn't help you bake the cake or build the house rafters. And, dropped out of context, a flash at a future step doesn't even give you a realistic image of what it will actually feel like to do that step. Between this step and that future step, you're going to build a lot more skills and you'll have a much deeper understanding of your project.

So yeah, maybe step 72 really would be terrifying if you had to time travel to it today. But your name isn't Marty McFly, and you have plenty of time to build the skills, muscle, and knowledge between today and step 72 so you will get it right.

Think of this like someone took six-year-old you and

dropped that poor child into the simplest day of your life today. It would be scary, overwhelming, and that small child would have no idea how to do a lot of the tasks that you can now do with your eyes closed. Because you've had a lot of steps between six and today to improve your skills and knowledge. Well, the same is true for you at step 7 and step 72. You'll be ready to figure it out when you get there.

As my grandma always said, "Don't borrow trouble from tomorrow, just do today."

Focus on the big picture of the project and don't torture yourself by trying to understand steps that you don't yet have a context for. At this point, as long as you know enough to understand your budget, your timeline, and most of the tools, supplies, and equipment, you're good to go.

As for all those small details? You'll figure those out as you go. This isn't some method I made up, it's called on the job learning, or learn as you go. And as we've already seen, it's the smartest way to take advantage of the way your brain works. (Stay tuned for even more brain hacking in the next few chapters!)

You don't have to know how to do the whole thing to take one step forward.

The best way to maintain the excited momentum you felt at the onset of your idea is to figure out the step in front of you. Then figure out the next step. And then the one after that. Rewind.

It's not like you're going in blindfolded. This is a project you know something about in a field you likely have some level of expertise, so you had at least a rough idea what the major phases of the project would be and probably a good idea what some of the smaller steps would be, even if you didn't know exactly how to do them.

For example, I didn't know exactly how to run water, sewer, and gas lines when I had the idea to build a house. I didn't know how to frame a wall, a window, or a rafter. But I did know that all those things were part of the process. And I was confident that I could watch someone doing these things in a tutorial video and replicate those steps.

Here's another way to think of this as it relates to our take-action strategies. When you follow someone through a how-to video, you automatically have this blind trust and confidence in them. You saw the evidence that they succeeded, and you trust they can now help you succeed. This complete stranger who probably looks about twelve years old, lives thousands of miles from you, and has just talked you into baking a lemon Bundt cake at midnight is awarded your full trust and attention.

It sounds bizarre when you break it down, but because you now know that their method uses psychology to successfully motivate you to action, and you can now use every golden morsel of their method to your advantage.

If you'll blindly follow that stranger out to your garage with a can of spray paint and the door of your refrigerator, why in the world wouldn't you have at least as much confidence that your skill and determination will take you all the way to your biggest goal? Give yourself at least as much credit as you give the strangers on the internet.

I know, I can't believe I had to say that out loud just now. But the truth is, we all needed to hear it.

Eyes on the prize, and on the step in front of you.

Quit borrowing future steps and turning them into today's problems.

Hard Work is Your Advantage

Let's dig a little deeper into this, because if we can debunk one of the big myths that makes us sometimes believe in a stranger more than we believe in ourselves, we'll make another huge stride in how confidently we launch into our projects.

When we hit a tough spot that makes us doubt our ability, one of the most common things we say is, "Maybe I'm just not cut out for this."

It's no real surprise that we feel this way. Other people look so much more capable and sure of themselves. Especially the people we see on social media. They get compliments like, "You're a natural born talent."

We've all done this. We witness someone at the top of their game in things like sports, music, or acting and it looks like they're born to do it. Their teachers and parents even have adorable little anecdotes like, "Justin used his baby bottle as a microphone." or "Tosha outran the family border collie when she was four."

This makes it so easy to attribute their excellence to a natural talent gifted to them at birth.

As it turns out though, this isn't true. These stars weren't born with ability, or even an advantage over you to develop it. Research says we're actually born with very few—if any—innate skills or talents. Even talents like having perfect pitch that were believed for years to be either present or not from a young age have now been proven to be teachable.

The research is conclusive—very few genetic characteristics give people a real advantage that couldn't be equaled with hard work.

You know what makes people so good at a thing that they look like they were born doing it? Practice and determination.

From Olympic gold to CEO of a Fortune 500 company, the people at the top got there through long hours of hard work. It wasn't all one happy success after another, either. They made a pile of mistakes along the way. They started over again and again. They set up a massive goal. Then they took one step forward, and repeated it, through success and setback.

Dozens of studies over the past few decades have proven that no can perform at a high level without experience or practice. In fact, even the most accomplished, natural looking successes needed about ten years of hard work before they became an expert in their field. I know you're thinking about some child prodigies, but even the most stand-out masters, like Bobby Fischer who became a chess grandmaster at only sixteen, had put in nine years of intensive study and practice by that age.

It may look like it came so naturally or that it was a true Cinderella story, but dig a little deeper and you'll repeatedly find that these heroes are yet another overnight success that came after years of hard work.

Hold on a minute though, if natural talent doesn't exist, why in the world do so many people dismiss major achievements with this label?

We want to believe in natural talent because it takes the pressure off us. It's an easy way out when the work is difficult. It's an easy way to quit when we're afraid we're failing. If we declare that we just don't have what it takes, we won't have to stretch our ability or challenge our minds. We play this excuse like a get-out-of-project-free card.

Studies show that if we're taught that a particular goal takes natural talent, we are more likely to procrastinate, not try very hard, be generally disinterested, or outright fail at it.

It's really too bad. We're doing ourselves (and everyone) a terrible disservice by pretending this myth is a reality. This is about more than you and your goals. Every time you say you're not cut out for something, your children or other people around you believe it, too. And it's just a matter of time before they look at someone at the top of their game and label it a natural talent they could never achieve. They take that myth and apply it to themselves. That's how feeling stuck becomes an epidemic.

How do you overcome this myth?

If you simply accept that a goal takes hard work to achieve, that alone will make all the difference. Simply acknowledging the hard work and dedication a top-level player put in can change our destiny. Believe effort can move the needle on our goal, and we'll give that goal everything we have.

It's astonishing what a big change such a little thing can make, isn't it?

You have a lot more control over your future than you think. And that means you're a lot stronger and a lot less stuck than you think. Hang up the myth of natural talent, and say hello to the reality that your effort and determination make all the difference.

Albert Einstein was asked near the end of his life how he thought of so many extraordinary ideas. He replied, almost surprised, "I spent nearly the whole of my life thinking of them!"

The biggest takeaway from all the research on this topic is that you can be good at whatever you want.

Beginner's Luck

Before we move on, I want to make sure you're ready for one weird effect of this one-step-at-a-time approach. It's not necessarily a bad thing, but it can take you by surprise.

Every step can feel a little like a new beginning. And because we know starting things is hard, you might mistake this weird feeling for a slow down or even a stuck feeling when that isn't what it is at all.

Here are some of the things that make you feel like you're beginning all over again:

The first step after a big mistake.

The first step of the day.

The first step with a new tool.

The first step after lunch.

The first step after vacation.

Or the first step of a new phase of the project.

Even now that you know some of the tricks for maintaining motivation, beginning again and again can feel uncomfortable.

I have a solution for all these beginnings—you just need

some beginner's luck.

Maybe you're the sort of person who has a four-leaf clover and a pair of lucky socks and maybe you're not. I'm not here to knock anything that boosts your confidence. But I am here to share an endless source of beginner's luck with you. I got it from my grandma, and there's plenty for everyone.

I can remember the exact weekend Grandma taught me to be lucky. Not just lucky rabbit foot lucky, but genuinely lucky at literally everything in life.

You should know, that in addition to being a master of luck, Grandma was a master of spoiling my brother JC and me. For every visit, she had our favorite foods ready for the asking. And no problem if I wanted chicken and JC wanted pork chops, she'd just make both. Black olives. Lemonade. Pineapple. Jelly donuts. Every weekend visit was a holiday feast.

We went for walks, watched the small-town baseball games—I was in it for the snow cones. In the evenings we did puzzles or played card games like solitaire, war, go fish, and JC's favorite, rummy.

I entertained myself with a puzzle or building card castles whenever they played rummy though, because it looked way too hard.

On this particular weekend (I was about six) I got restless, interrupting them, picking at my brother, and being generally annoying. I felt left out. I whined, "Someday, when I'm big, I wanna play rummy with you."

Grandma shuffled the cards and dealt me in.

I pushed back from the table, eyes wide and mouth

dumping all the excuses about why I absolutely could not play. "I can't. I don't know why sometimes you put the same colors here, and sometimes both colors. I don't get when you pick up from the upside-down pile or the messy one. What's a discard? It's too hard. I don't know how. I can't!"

JC agreed enthusiastically that I definitely could *not* do this. I should keep playing puzzles. I was absolutely too little—and probably not smart enough. I should definitely just go away.

My F3 response had me ready to dash out of the room in tears. It may not have been a life-or-death situation, but I felt a flood of anxiety. I had failed at enough things in my six years to know that it felt bad to fail. It felt bad to be too small, too weak, too slow, or too confused to keep up with a game. I knew for sure I didn't want to feel that way, and I kept arguing with Grandma. JC agreed at every point, determined to have the game—and Grandma—back to himself.

Grandma put her palm up. "Cara, can you hold seven cards?" (Grandma knew our trick about the easy first step.)

"Yes, but I can't— "

Palm up again, looking directly in my nervous little eyes, "Can you hold seven cards?"

I nodded.

"You'll figure out the rest as we go," and she said that like it was gospel truth.

I started that first hand with three aces, and somehow didn't suspect that was a grandma setup through and through. Within minutes I figured out when to pick up a card, and how to decide what to throw away. Some of the stuff I'd learned playing solitaire came in handy. I did some things wrong, and even JC let me have some do-overs. I figured it out.

We played until after bedtime. And, I won.

"Beginner's luck!" Grandma said, throwing down her cards like she was mourning her loss.

The next morning, we picked raspberries. My bucket was the fullest. Grandma said it was beginner's luck, even though it wasn't really the first time I'd picked berries.

I helped peel cucumbers and didn't even hurt myself once. I washed all the dishes and my shirt was still mostly dry, if you didn't count the sleeves. I was on a roll. Everything I did that weekend turned to pure gold. Beginner's luck, my grandma said over and over again.

But I had failed at enough things to know this couldn't last. I would have bad luck again. Probably a lot of it. My beginner's luck felt like a fluke. And I didn't want it to be. I wanted to feel that good—that confident and capable—forever.

So, I asked Grandma, "What if we could keep beginner's luck forever?"

Grandma didn't pause, just looked me straight in the eyes and said, "Well of course you can keep beginner's luck. Just keep beginning."

It sounds simple because it is simple. Keep trying new things. Keep going for it. Keep taking those blind steps forward and know you'll figure it out as you go.

I've never stopped believing in my grandma's version of beginner's luck. The kind of luck that follows the idea that the harder I work, the luckier I get. To create luck, to create success, all you have to do is begin. Because when it all shakes out in the wash, you'll be a lot better at most things that you thought you'd be. And the rest, you'll figure out as you go.

I played rummy with JC and Grandma hundreds of nights after that. And I'd give a lot to sit around the table with them again, laughing as we slap the cards down fast in a lighting round. I still have a deck of my grandma's cards. The ink is worn completely off each card in the spot where her thumb swiped against it for the next deal.

We've all heard that the harder you work, the luckier you get. And in honor of my grandma let's add, the more we begin the more beginner's luck we get.

CHAPTER SEVEN

Worst Case Scenario

*BECAUSE A THING SEEMS DIFFICULT
FOR YOU, DO NOT THINK IT IMPOSSIBLE.
- MARCUS AURELIUS*

Before we dig into the next few chapters, let's talk about what's in them. Because I made a promise way back at the beginning of this book, and I intend to stick to it.

Let's start with a quick recap of how we got here: This book is about getting unstuck. It's about taking the first step toward whatever goal you want to reach right now. It's about how sometimes you feel so stuck in place that you don't know how to begin. And it's about how you can end that cycle forever.

This book is meant to get you moving. And you're well on your way there.

We've already covered the psychology of feeling stuck, and we set up the simple foundation steps to create your own goal play button. The three easy steps are set the scene, take blind action, and rewind as needed. Now I want to make good on another promise I made to you. It's time for a touch of Hollywood-style special effects.

This is where things get even more interesting. Because mixing Hollywood with brain science creates one heck of a blockbuster reel. I'm ready for it, and so are you. Tuck in with some popcorn and let the show begin.

Part of the magic behind movies and how-to videos is how we can suspend all disbelief and just enjoy the results of the final cut. It's the same with how-to videos. Even the most basic one has dozens of outtakes and hours of trashed footage for every minute of final screen play. That final video isn't even close to real-time action. It's more like a trailer for a DIY project. And that means the project looks and feels way easier than it's going to be in real life.

None of this is a secret. We know from the moment we press play that every video has taken full advantage of creative edits and special effects. We enter into this world willingly. Which means, of course, we can just as willingly watch everything with a completely different eye.

Let's pull back the theater curtains and bring up the house lights. Because in order to identify how to sprinkle these effects into our own goal-reaching habits, we have to look that stunt double straight in the eye.

Here are a few of the things we all know and accept as we watch a video.

We know that a great big mess is hidden offscreen.

We know it took 25 tries to get a difficult step right.

We know that a photo montage sped us through the boring parts.

We even know about the time-lapse.

The weird part of all of this? We don't mind the trickery at all. I mean, it was pretty obvious that shingling your roof or sewing a winter coat was going to take you longer than the two-minute video. No problem. Who wants to watch endless fails or the actual day-long process in real time? Definitely no one. Now and then we do enjoy a few choice fails in the cut scenes reel, or maybe one or two giggle-worthy attempts along the way. But all in all, that finished video is clean, pristine, and barely resembles reality. We're perfectly fine with that, and the reasons why are simple.

We have a short attention span, and a high opinion of our ability.

Because of this, we never let reality get in the way of a good story—or in this case, a good how-to video. This mindset makes the simplest recipe our favorite recipe.

This is also why your new TV, microwave, and even your brand-new car come with a high-gloss card labeled "Quick Start Guide." The instruction manual writers know you want to skip to the good parts, so they give you the print equivalent of an overly-produced how-to video.

We prefer the simplest form of any explanation, so we sign up for the over-simplified videos and let our brain revel in the effects.

But here's a really important question: Does willingly signing ourselves up for this brain trickery actually help us get started on a project?

Yes, it actually does. As a matter of fact, these effects are vital to our success. They're part of the magic that pulls us into the video in the first place. And the reason they work is because they're perfectly aligned with the way the more primitive part of your brain already works.

I bet you know where we're going to take this next.

You guessed it. We're going to use this to our advantage.

Let's sprinkle these special effects into our project plan, because in order to use our how-to video strategies to their best advantage, we need our brain to love every second of it. It'll be no surprise to you that the next few chapters are about how to make the best use of this. We'll maximize your success by mixing modern psychology with the primitive habits already built into your brain. This mix will make your first step irresistible. Let's get moving with some radical new ideas that will forever change the way you live and work.

Can You Live With That?

Our first special effect originated on our construction site. It's one of the weird little tricks I used to break my kids out of an analysis paralysis state whenever they froze up. I started using this really early in the process, when we were still covered in mud and struggling through the foundation work. And I definitely didn't fully understand why it worked until much later in the project. Sometimes you just do what works and sort out the details later.

This special effect inspired trick saved us a lot of time. With an incredibly short nine-month deadline to build our entire house, we couldn't afford to waste a single minute.

A couple weeks into our house project, just after Christmas, I saw my kids freeze up on the construction site for the first time. (The irony is not lost on me that it was about 25 degrees outside so our toes were as frozen as our minds.) Even at this early stage of our project, we had made a lot of progress for amateurs. We had cleared the site, marked the spot for our house, and I even found a guy to dig a footer for us.

The footer, in case building houses isn't your thing, is just a trench that's about two feet wide and three or four feet deep, give or take, the same size and shape as your house. You can think of it like a house footprint. In our case the footer was a big rectangle. Picture a big, muddy rectangular trench in the middle of a field. That's where this story begins. It's about four in the afternoon, after work and school. It's freezing cold weather and on scene you see a mom and four kids staring down into that trench—possibly with a look of dismay on their rosy red faces.

Oh, and we were also dressed more like we were hanging out at a Halloween hay ride than a construction site. That's how out of our league we were on this project, we didn't even know what an appropriate outfit would be. I was wearing dangling earrings, for goodness sakes.

Anyhow, the improper attire extended all the way to our footwear. We didn't own work boots or even rain boots. We were each wearing our oldest tennis shoes, which means a couple of the kids were wearing shoes a half-size too small. And as a cheap attempt to waterproof our toes, we'd put plastic bread bags over our stocking feet before we put on the old shoes.

UNSTUCK

Our next step before we could fill that footer with concrete and build a house on top of it was to prop long pieces of metal rods (called rebar) a couple inches from the bottom of the trench. A job we were all trying to avoid, and not only because we'd have to stand ankle deep in freezing mud to do it.

We'd watched a handful of tutorials, and made our best attempt to draw each step onto a Post-it note. Because remember, this was 2007 and still years before we'd all be watching videos on our phones.

Even after all that advanced prep work, when we all stared down into that muddy trench, no one wanted to make the first move.

The real problem was that we didn't know how to do it. Every step and supply for this job was completely foreign to us. The rebar, the three-inch-tall plastic chairs that were supposed to do the propping, and even the full purpose of this step might as well have come from some alien planet.

As I reviewed our neon pink Post-it notes, the usual rush of F3 responses were on full display. Eyes wide, breathing rapid, heart galloping along, nostrils flared, my brain wildly running through the possible escape routes. And at the same time the more logical modern part of my brain was reminding me that we couldn't escape, not with our tight deadline and how badly we needed this house.

What you have right there is the perfect recipe for a sort of quicksand stuck feeling that locks you tight in place feeling panicked and helpless. My kids were experiencing the same sort of reaction to this modern-day monster that's otherwise known as a really difficult step.

For the same reason that we can always see other people's faults before we see our own, I recognized what was happening in my kids long before I recognized it in myself. So, whenever I noticed the kids were slowly drawing circles in the mud or sawdust with the tips of their old shoes, avoiding eye contact, and making a list of 75 other things we could do instead of doing the thing in front of us, I learned to ask a single question.

You can think of this question as a shortcut to creating your own glossy quick start guide.

I would ask, "What's our worst case scenario?"

That's it. A really simple question that focused our thoughts.

Of course, the first couple of times I asked this question, it wasn't much help at all. I said, "What's our worst case scenario?"

Jada said, "We could freeze to death."

Hope said, "We could impale ourselves on a piece of rebar."

Drew said, "An airplane engine could fall out of the sky and crush us."

Roman said, "I want cookies."

I realized then that I had to clarify the rules of this game by saying, "What's our worst case scenario *that's actually likely to happen.*"

And their answer was the same almost every single time. None of those wild one-in-a-million things were going to happen. The most likely disaster was that we'd do it wrong. Then we'd have to take it apart, and do it again until we got it right. And while that may not sound like a barrel of laughs, it's definitely more fun than being crushed by an airplane engine. Or to put it simply, getting something wrong isn't such a big deal.

Next, I'd ask them, "Can you live with that?"

Every single time the answer was, "Yes."

Well, to be specific it was more like, "Yes. We did that 24 times yesterday and we're still breathing."

Then I'd say, "Hand me those rebar props and let's give this a go."

We failed at that step, by the way. Many, many times. First because the rebar prop chairs tipped over. Then because as the ground thawed the chairs sank in the mud. Then because working until midnight by headlights is a huge challenge when you're four feet deep in a dark trench. The only thing lit up by those headlights were our frozen noses and annoyed scowls when we tripped over the rebar, knocking it all over for the umpteenth time.

We went home discouraged that night.

But the next day we showed up at the site with new ideas. We tried them, and we figured it out. We gathered the flattest rocks we could find and used them as a little base under our chairs, or in some places instead of chairs. We passed that inspection, poured the footer. And then froze up with paralysis again when 1,500 blocks arrived on site.

As we were all staring down at a wheelbarrow of wet mortar surrounded by a tower of foundation blocks, I asked the kids, "What's our worst case scenario here?"

And they answered, "That we'll do it wrong and have to do it over."

We could live with that.

We set that first block. Later we realized it wasn't quite right and knocked it out with a sledge hammer. And then did the same thing one more time before we got it right.

We went through this sequence over and over again until we had a house.

Let's press pause right there and talk about how that simple question worked with our already well-established brain pathways to get us moving, and how all of this relates to the special effects we find in how-to videos.

I've mentioned analysis paralysis several times, and it's kind of self-explanatory, but let's talk about how that fits here. When we go into F3 mode, our brain automatically runs a risk analysis to narrow down our options. And because that primitive part of our brain has one single job—to keep us alive—it creates overly dramatic scenarios to try to get us moving quickly to the safest option.

According to your primitive brain, when you're faced with something new and scary the safest option is almost always running back to the cave. Because anytime you're out in the open, there might be tigers. Or you could fall into quicksand. The river may flood. Or the sky might fall. Go back to the cave and roll the stone door into place.

When you approach a modern task that makes your tummy flutter with anxiety, your brain does the same thing a human brain did 10,000 years ago when something scary popped up.

We approached the trench and our brains sent out emergency warnings that looked something like: You could freeze to death. You could impale yourself on the rebar. An airplane engine could crush you. You should just go home, eat cookies, and binge Netflix, save this house building idea for some other day. Way too often, you listen to this primitive brain. And you know what happens when you do.

Just like that, you're stuck.

Unless you're following a how-to video. Then you're a lot more likely to plow straight ahead without a single worry over saber-toothed tigers or stray airplane engines. And the reason this works is much simpler than you'd expect.

A how-to video narrows the playing field to keep that overly dramatic, primitive part of your brain under control. This works because despite the movie magic, the host never exactly claims that everything is going to go perfectly. And that's important because your primitive brain would body slam anyone who suggested the risk analysis resulted in a 100 percent safety evaluation. Your primitive brain is preprogrammed. It's automatic. Fight it and you'll lose way more often than you'll win. Fight it and you'll be exhausted, anxious, and overwhelmed.

But if you instead just narrow the playing field, you'll set it loose in that much smaller range of thought. Which it's happy to let you do. Because another thing your primitive brain tends to do is to always look for the easiest way out. You know that quick start guide is around here somewhere, and the second you find it you're ready to go.

A video tutorial works the exact same way. It tosses out a handful of sweetened risks like candy at a parade, and your brain grabs them all up. The video may casually list some of the things that could go wrong, or even show you some simple, low-drama, low-stakes examples of things that went a little off the rails for them. Almost always these minor mistakes will appear with a few laughs to reinforce that the worst case scenario is so survivable it'll even be fun.

Can you see how this is the same thing I was doing with my simple question? "What's our worst case scenario here?"

I narrowed our primitive brains to focus on the playing field we created when I limited the answers to the things that would actually be likely to happen in our exact setting. And we reinforced how low stakes those possibilities were by asking, "Can you live with that?"

Here's another way to think of this.

If you try to help your toddler gain confidence by letting them choose anything they want to wear on a winter day when it's ten degrees outside, what will happen? They will invariably pull out their favorite grass skirt and coconut bra. And if you argue, the whole day goes from bad to worse and everyone's confidence takes a stomping.

Instead, you let them choose what they want to wear but only from three pre-filtered options that are appropriate for the weather. Then you declare, "Look what a perfect outfit little Harry chose today!" *wink*wink*

This is one of the ways the structure of a how-to video offers much needed structure to the alarmist parts of our primitive brain. And this is how we can mimic that structure to get moving on our own goals.

It works. Not only in how to videos, but in the goals we set up ourselves. The key here is to simply identify and minimize your worst case scenario.

It sounds easy because it is easy.

Because it works with the way our brain is already set up

to work. I know you're all ready to go out and try this, but wait just one minute, because we have to address one other direction this question could take you. What if the opposite thing happens? What if when you ask the question, "What's our worst case scenario here?" And you can't live with the answer?

There are legitimately scary answers to this question in some situations and no one wants to live with the worst case of those. Here are some examples of times we got an answer we didn't like.

On our construction site when I was prepping to cut some large beams with a new saw, or run our gas lines, the answers were different. The kids weren't exaggerating when they replied, "You could cut off your left hand." or "You could blow us all up." These weren't wild ideas drummed up by an overly dramatic primitive brain, they were real possibilities. And when our analysis detects actual risk, we have to pay attention.

Back when I told you to dive into your easy first step quickly, that didn't mean to be reckless or to stop planning and researching all together. It meant that in order to keep your momentum up and your learning efficient, you instead research and learn as you go. Specifically, you should take the steps to reduce every risk as it's identified.

When I picked up a new saw or began using an old saw in a new way, I first learned the correct method and took the necessary safety precautions for each cut. For the gas lines, I watched a lot of videos and then talked to the city inspector, the gas company, and various people in the aisles of Home Depot. I learned, I took the precautions, and then I carefully moved forward.

And that's the very important story of why I still have a left hand and never blew anyone up.

Evaluate True Risk

Keep in mind that not all risk is physical. Your projects may involve financial or social risk instead. Either way, the primitive part of your brain is going to react the same way to what it over-simplifies as a perceived threat to your survival.

Let's look at the way a man in Cambodia managed a massive DIY project that began with how-to videos and involved significant financial, social, and physical risk.

That man's name is Paen Long. He's in his thirties and lives in a small Cambodian village near the Vietnam border. The impoverished village had struggled for years after a communist regime killed almost two million people in four years. Everyone was focused on survival, so it wasn't a place where people dreamed big dreams. At least not until Long proved that he could do the impossible.

For about three years, Long secretly watched YouTube videos late at night. He had a dream of flying his own plane, but he didn't want anyone to know. After all, he certainly wasn't the type of person who could ever expect to buy a plane, or even a ticket for a plane ride.

Just meeting basic needs had been a struggle his entire life. His parents worked in the rice fields, and when he was only seven years old Long started working as a cattle herder at his neighbor's farm to make money to help his family. He couldn't read or write, and his future as a farm hand seemed set. But then one day while he was out with the cattle, he saw a helicopter fall from the sky. That moment changed everything for him.

The small boy ran to the crash site along with hundreds of other villagers. Everyone was terrified of the broken mass of metal, but seven-year-old Long wasn't scared at all. In fact, he felt happy and hopeful. The idea that people could fly in a machine captivated him. Because it meant that one day *he* could fly in a machine.

Every single day after that, he was looking to the sky and imagining what it would be like to fly. He thought about it so often that he even had dreams about flying. Even though he spent year after year working on the cattle farm, he knew without any doubt that he'd build a plane one day. He could see that for himself in perfect detail.

While going to engineering school wasn't possible, he did learn to read and write. Eventually he even trained to be an auto mechanic and establish his own business. He got married and had a child of his own. Still, every day he looked to the sky, and every night he dreamed of his own flying machines.

He knew though that everyone would laugh if they knew about his wild dream, so he kept the secret to himself. It won't surprise you at all that everything changed on the day he started watching how-to videos.

"In the beginning, I typed in the word, *Jet*," Long said.

Then he would watch flight simulations, and takeoff and landing sequences. Throughout every video, he imagined he was the one doing the flying.

Do you recognize this? It's visualization at its finest! This is how the most successful people in the world set up their goals. And it works.

Eventually, Long found videos about aircraft factories. And while he didn't even speak the language in the videos, he could still understand the building process. He decided that both jets and helicopters were out of his reach, but when he found designs of a WWII Japanese plane, he went out to his shop and used recycled materials to start building his first plane. He worked at night at first so no one would make fun of him. But as the project took shape, so did his confidence.

First, he told his wife about the project. And while he worked from the cockpit of his plane—a cockpit he'd made from an old gas container—other people in the village soon heard about the plane project too. They watched him work, but with no vision in their own minds of what was possible, they wondered if he'd lost his mind.

Even when people talked about him behind his back, Long continued, making his pilot's seat by chopping the legs off a plastic chair and securing it in the cockpit. He worked late into the night and kept his dream alive, ignoring all the criticism.

Finally, one March afternoon, the only thing left to do was test his creation. Many people were still mocking him, but a few were in awe of his idea and especially of his determination to turn it into a reality. Long didn't worry about what anyone else thought as he pushed his plane onto a dirt road leading toward the rice paddy fields. Then, exactly like he'd been doing in his dreams since he was seven years old, he did the impossible.

With a motorbike helmet as his only safety device, Long

fired up the propeller of his DIY airplane. In front of about 200 people from his village, he rumbled down the dirt road and lifted into the air. He estimated that he reached about 160 feet into the air before he crashed unceremoniously to the ground—probably because his DIY plane was pretty heavy.

What some people might call a setback or failure instead became Long's fuel for new ideas. He said he cried after that crash. Maybe because some people were still laughing at his dream. And maybe because it hadn't gone exactly right. We have to guess that some of those tears were even because crashing a plane hurts a lot. But Long was also crying in victory. After a lifetime of dreaming, he had built a real flying machine and lifted himself into the air.

Let's consider what else Long must have been feeling at this moment. There's no doubt his F3 response was firing like mad. His body and mind were primed to face danger. But he could see in his mind his perfect takeoff and landing—something he'd visualized over and over again. He believed with everything in him that he would soar effortlessly through the sky. He moved quickly into his first step, leaping into the plastic seat and taking off down that makeshift runway without a moment to reconsider.

But there was a point where he had to ask himself the risk assessment questions. And from the looks of things, these questions felt a lot more real after the first flight than they had before it.

After a crash landing, it's a great time to evaluate.

What's my worst case scenario here? And can I live with that?

Weigh Risk Against Benefit

The worst case scenario of a plane crash is definitely not something an overly dramatic primitive brain has to make up. It's a really big deal. It's life or death. But in this case, and in many cases, a life-or-death risk isn't necessarily a reason to stop what you're doing. People accept this worst case scenario every single day.

People climb mountains, or drive race cars over 200 mph, or blast off into space. People use dangerous equipment and work with deadly animals. Even in the most risky situation, asking this question is never meant to stop you completely.

This question is meant to help you evaluate two things. First, is the level of actual risk acceptable to you? (Actual risk, not the elevated overly-dramatic risk.) And second, are you taking all the precautions and armed with top-level knowledge and skills to prevent a catastrophic crash?

In Paen Long's case, his wife and two small children had an impact on his answer to these questions. They had to evaluate the financial, social, and physical risk of this project. Long was investing a disproportionate amount of his financial resources and time in his dream. It also had a social effect on him and on his family, because so many people thought a flying machine was a crazy dream.

Long could not give up his lifelong dream of flying, it had become part of who he was. He decided it was worth his financial, time, and social risk. But he also decided he would need to adjust his plan to stay as safe as possible for his family. This led to a compromise with his wife.

He would build a different kind of flying machine. This time, it would be a sea plane, with the idea that crashing in the water would be at least a little less dangerous. Immediately, he took one easy first step to begin building his sea plane.

Long did this even though he lives 120 miles from the ocean and wasn't sure in that first moment how he would get it to the water once he finished. Long didn't worry about step 702 just yet. All his focus was on step one, and he would figure out the next steps one at a time.

Following the same model of the YouTube videos that had moved him to his first action, Long pressed play on his new goal.

I know this entire airplane story might sound a little nuts to you. It's pretty extreme. But big projects that feel impossible are how the biggest innovations happen. This much drive is bound to not only change one man's life, but I won't be surprised if Long discovers some revolutionary design for air travel. A creative mind lighting up with creative energy sparks even more creative potential.

Big leaps like this create big change. And the more you and your family and friends take on projects that at first glance look impossible, the more natural they will feel. Success on one project, even a small one, brings new confidence and bigger dreams to the next one.

Maybe that's why this airplane thing doesn't feel all that radical to me. I can remember the summer when my mom and dad found some basic plans in a magazine that showed how to build a motorized glider—which is basically a mini airplane—and they decided to build one using an old lawnmower engine. Sound a little crazy?

I didn't think so. Because my parents were always doing projects. And because they were usually successful projects, I believed this one would be too. They talked about it for weeks. Carefully calculating how much weight our little glider would hold so we would know which family members could pair up in it and who would be waving from the back yard. I could definitely imagine myself soaring over the house, my little dog yipping up at us from his favorite spot near the swing set.

My parents never built that glider, but they did dig (with shovels) a full-sized in-ground, indoor swimming pool in our back yard. Scooping the first shovel of dirt mere days after mom mentioned she'd like a small greenhouse shed for her plants, which eventually morphed into a shed nearly as big as our house to hold a pool instead of plants.

Using the same efficient model as a how-to video, my parents started and finished projects.

Are You Living Your Worst Case Scenario?

The press play effect gets us moving.

It works for the small things like baking a Bundt cake, and for the wild ideas at the opposite end of the spectrum that require a larger risk like building an airplane or a rocket. This works not only in how-to videos, but in the goals we set up ourselves. That's not all, though—the benefits of this amazing special effect go even deeper.

Now that we've gone to some pretty extreme levels, let's dial this back to look at how this exact same method is

UNSTUCK

effective in any situation where you're uncertain or anxious about taking a step. Not a step outside the space shuttle or anything massive, but any small step outside your comfort zone.

After my kids and I built our house and had been living there for a couple years, my oldest son Drew had the opportunity to go to college in Fairbanks Alaska. To say my outdoorsy, adventurous boy was excited is an understatement. He talked so enthusiastically about all things Alaska that the whole family briefly considered buying a sled dog to hang out at Inkwell Manor. He was obsessed. But then, the night before he was supposed to fly out, that old F3 response kicked in hard.

One minute he was packing his climbing gear into his suitcase, and in the blink of an eye he had changed his mind and decided he would rather stay home and continue at a local college. Nerves jittering, he paced back and forth in his room and asked me, "What if I get all the way up to Alaska and I hate it? What if school is too hard? What if the cold is more than I can take? What if it's just awful?"

You already guessed what I did. I asked him, "What's our worst case scenario? What will you do if any of those things happen?"

He stopped and thought a few seconds. "I'd have to live at Inkwell Manor."

I raised my eyebrows. "Drew, that's where you live now. So obviously you can live with your worst case scenario. In fact, if you stay here, you'll be accepting your worst case scenario permanently. Go to Alaska. If you hate it, come home"

He went. He skied. He hiked. He climbed mountains.

He even climbed ice walls. And he also attended some college classes between those things. He did the big thing and not one of those overly-dramatic worst case scenarios that he had imagined in that last minute of fear ended up sending him packing back home. Instead, he will have amazing memories of that bold move to Alaska for the rest of his life.

Looking for a little Hollywood magic to kick your projects into high gear? Use this special effect to get yourself up and moving.

The key here is identifying and minimizing your worst case scenario. This sounds easy because it is easy. It works not because it's a kind of magic trick, but because it works within the boundaries of how your brain is already set up to work.

Narrow down your freak-out parameters and create a quick start guide for your actions by focusing on your big goal and the major steps to reach it. You can do amazing things. And this special effect will keep you on track until you reach success.

CHAPTER EIGHT

The Yet Principle

TO SEE THINGS IN THE SEED, THAT IS GENIUS.
- LAO TZU

Setting and hitting goals of all sizes takes practice. I've discovered one tiny perspective shift that sets you up for a better start and a guaranteed finish. It's a little thing that I've always done because my parents and grandparents did it. In fact, it seemed like such a logical way to see things that I assumed everyone did it. But when I was almost finished building my house, I realized that this approach to hitting goals was actually fairly unique.

As you might have guessed, this cinema-ready special effect is a huge part of what makes the press play effect work. And you want to know the best part? It's just a word. That's right, one single, tiny word that will forever change your goal setting strategy.

The word is: Yet.

Let me tell you about the exact moment when I realized that the way I use this little word is not only unique, but incredibly valuable.

The kids and I had already built most of what we called *the big stuff* for our house. We had a foundation, walls, rough plumbing, sheetrock, windows, and even hardwood flooring. We'd worked our tails off but we were running out of time. Remember, we had only a nine-month construction loan to build our entire house, so we were pretty much behind schedule and in danger of failing from the start.

And we weren't only running out of time, we were also running out of money. This meant I couldn't afford some of the really basic but essential household things like countertops. Obviously, my house wouldn't pass the bank or city inspections without countertops in the kitchen and bathrooms, so I had to get really creative with a solution.

On a Wednesday afternoon, mere weeks before our deadline, I made a surprise announcement to my kids, "Our only option is to make the countertops ourselves, and we're going to make them out of concrete."

Desperate times, desperate measures.

That same afternoon, a good friend named Eric stopped by. Eric had heard that we were in a tough spot with the build and offered to help wherever we needed him. This was the first time he had seen our crazy construction site—or any construction site for that matter. He told us up front that he didn't know anything about building houses, but the kids and I didn't care one bit. Neither did we.

We imagined his extra hands being just the thing to help

us pull off our impossible deadline. Until, that is, I realized Eric and I had vastly different perspectives when it came to doing tasks that we had no idea how to do.

Those DIY concrete countertops were the biggest project on my list, so I took Eric into the bathroom and pointed at the pile of scrap lumber he could use. I explained what a finished concrete countertop was supposed to look like, and then I pointed at a series of the little Post-it notes I'd stuck to the wall above the vanity. Each of those notes had a rough sketch of one possible way a person might make a frame for a concrete countertop. By frame, I just mean a wooden thing that would hold the wet concrete. Once it hardened, we would remove the sides of the frame and Voila, concrete countertops!

This is a good time to remind you that this was 2008. So, what we now recognize as a smartphone didn't exist. (And wouldn't be widely used until 2012.) That means we couldn't prop up a phone playing a how-to video while we worked. We had to just figure stuff out as we went. Sometimes we went in with a vague memory of the video we'd watched the night before on our shared family computer, and sometimes we didn't even have that advantage.

YouTube didn't have any clear videos about pour-in-place concrete countertops. I couldn't find articles or books about it either. I finally ordered a book about concrete finishing techniques from a growing book site called Amazon. And because every idea sparks more creative ideas, that book helped me brainstorm the framing process too.

The way I saw it, my book, Post-it notes, and a lot of trial and error were more than enough to get this job underway.

I left Eric to work on the countertop frame while I returned to another bathroom where I had already mixed mortar to lay some tile.

What I thought would happen was this: I thought Eric would lay out a bunch of pieces of wood, rearrange them, start over, then finally nail it all together when he figured out a workable way to make a frame.

You've probably already guessed that's not at all what happened.

Less than five minutes later I was measuring a diagonal tile cut when Eric appeared in the doorway and said, "I don't know how to build that."

I blinked. Several times. I waited. I titled my head, listening. I blinked some more. I was waiting for Eric to say the last word of his sentence. But he didn't. He didn't say anything else. He didn't seem to know the little three letter word that is supposed to end any sentence that starts with either "I can't" or "I don't know how."

So, I told him the cold, hard truth. "I don't know how to build that either...." But I said it differently. It was a small difference, but it changed everything. My sentence ended the right way. It ended with that all important three-letter word: *yet*.

I said, "I don't know how to build that either, yet." And then I went on. "But give me a few minutes in there with that pile of wood and I'll figure it out."

It was Eric's turn to blink. Then he asked if there was something different he could help with. I offered to let him use the wet saw to cut tile for me (Even though that's definitely my favorite part.) I took him into the attic and told him

UNSTUCK

we needed a knee wall built for the tankless hot water heater. He shook his head. Shook his head again. And then again. Nope. Not that. And not that one either.

I didn't stop there. I showed him the garbage disposal—which came with detailed instructions. The stack of toilets in the garage. A pedestal sink.

Every single time, Eric said, "I don't know how to do that." And every single time he left off that last, essential word: *Yet.* I don't know how to do that, *YET.*

Boom

That's when it hit me.

This is why people had been looking at me like I was crazy. All these people at the hardware store, at the permit office, random neighbors and friends, they all think in an entirely different way than I do. They all think you have to know how to do something before you start it. And instead, I think you have to start something before you'll know how to do it. Think about that. Two types of people.

One type thinks they have to know how to do something before they start it.

And the other type thinks you have to start something before you'll know how to do it.

One of these types of people keeps putting projects off until "someday" and the other type actually does the project—starts it, figures it out, and finishes it. And the only difference between these two types of people is the slight perspective difference they get from one little three letter word: *yet*. Here's another way to look at how this can hold you back.

If you only do the types of projects that you know how

to do, then the best you can hope for is to stay where you are. You're treading water. Staying still. And that idea of staying still and not making your life any better—that's not what you're here for, is it?

You know you can do more than what you're doing now. You know you can have a better life than you have now. That's why you're here. And you're right. You can. It's easier than you think. And the mindset shift you get from this three-letter word is where the special effect magic begins.

You're Already a Puzzle Solver

Let's start by identifying the effect this word has on you, and then we'll get into the details of how to set it up on purpose in your goals.

Adding *yet* to the end of any sentence that begins with "I can't" or I don't know how to" actually changes the way you see yourself. Instead of seeing yourself as someone who takes a step back and chooses a simpler goal, you immediately see yourself as the type of person who figures things out.

That little word lights up a neuropathway in your brain like the trunk of a tree. The heat from that trunk ignites new ideas all along the pathway until you have a whole collection of possibilities sprouting out like branches. This idea tree is what sets you on fire with "what ifs" at the beginning of a project. One idea ignites another and having so many options increases your confidence as well as your rate of success.

Because our purpose here is to always work directly with

the way your brain is already set up to work, it'll be no surprise to you when I say that this happens automatically and with no effort from you.

You can try it with a simple idea right now.

Say out loud, "I don't know how to chisel my name on a rock."

There's a finality to that statement, isn't there? A shoulder shrugging moment that's a complete halt to your potential career as a rock chiseler.

Now try the other way. Say, "I don't know how to chisel my name on a rock, yet." You can whisper if you're worried about looking weird. Say it. "I don't know how to chisel my name on a rock, yet."

Even if this is 100 percent true. If you've never chiseled your name on a rock before, your brain will try to solve the puzzle for you automagically. (Automagically = your innate ability to figure things out so smoothly that it feels like magic.) Your brain will start searching the things you have done in your life for possible applications to this new task.

You'll think of random tools you've seen or even used before that might work to get your name on that rock. Maybe a screwdriver, a stick, a chisel, a shard of glass, or a random piece of metal. Then you might wonder if you could just scrape against the rock or if you'll need to use another object to hit the first object. Maybe you'll think of a smaller rock, a hammer, or your TV remote.

Some of these ideas would successfully carve your name in a rock, others would fail. But each one of them is a little branch of brightly lit neurons in your brain trying to figure this out. It works brilliantly and efficiently every time for every person. Your brain instantly sees you as the type of person who figures things out. And do you know why you can so easily see yourself that way?

Because you were born as that type of a person. You were born not knowing how to do a single thing. Your brain wasn't stressed out over that, it didn't hold you back from the things you didn't know how to do or tell you to stay in your lane. If your brain was designed to hold you to the things you already knew how to do, you'd still be flat in a crib sucking your thumb.

You're not. That's because you are the type of person who can figure things out. We all are. And we've proven this over and over again.

Now here's the best part. Once you reboot this valuable mindset that you were born with, every single goal you ever imagine will be within your reach. You will become the type of person who can do hard things.

To prove this, let's rewind to a very small version of brand-new baby you in your crib. You watched people standing on two feet and getting around really fast. They were touching things you were curious about, things you'd like to get your slobbery little hands on. That set off a little fire in your brain and you started working out how you might get up on your little feet and take some steps.

But watching other people walk wasn't enough for you to really learn how to do it. Learning the names of the muscles, and bones or technicalities of balance and coordination wouldn't have done the trick either. The only way you were going to learn how to do it, was to start trying to doing it. Sound familiar?

I told you. You already know how to use this mindset. You did it when you were a kid. It's simple: I don't know how to do this yet, but I'll keep trying things until I figure it out.

You got up onto those wee-small feet, balanced, and took those steps. You did all of this when the only thing you had to start with was the idea that you'd like to do it. That's it. You set a goal, you imagined yourself doing it, and then you kept trying different things until you did it. Naturally, this wasn't easy.

Sometimes you fell flat on your face. You had to practice some of the skills more than once before you got it all to work together. You had to build some muscle. You practiced some of the movements and balance in a crawl. Little by little, you got the motions down. After a while, it was easy. Eventually so easy that you didn't even have to think about any of the details to just push up and do it. And you didn't stop there.

You saw someone jump, use a fork, pour a glass of milk, draw a picture. When someone set a box of crayons in front of you the first time, you didn't wait to learn the names of all the colors or understand why crayon friction against paper made a mark. You grabbed one, and you did everything with it—including taking a bite of it and coloring on the walls. You tried out everything you could think of, and each time you used some of the skills you'd already learned and mastered and combined them with a few new things. The drawing muscles helped you hold a spoon. The walking muscles helped you jump. And run. You used this perspective to set your goals thousands of times. Until one day, something terrible happened.

You're the Type of Person Who Tries

You tried a new thing, fell flat on your butt like you always do when you try new things. But this time, instead of Mom and Dad cheering you on, the kids on the playground laughed at you. They said you were the worst ball player or rope jumper or singer they had ever seen. How you reacted may surprise you.

What they said, it didn't matter to you, not at first. You were curious enough and your mom and dad had filled you with enough confidence to keep trying things. Maybe you wouldn't try singing on the playground again, but you would leap right into other things that you had no idea how to do yet.

Until, one day, the terrible thing happened again. And again. This is when you started to worry you wouldn't fit in with the group. You worried all those people laughing at you wouldn't be your friend. Which sounds like a small thing on the surface, but to those primitive parts of your brain, this is huge.

Our primitive brain tells us that we have to remain part of a group. Take a small step outside of the group rules, and our F3 response has us scrambling to do whatever it takes to hold on to the safety of our group. Because if we're tossed out of the cave, we'll die. Our cave brothers and sisters needed the tribe to survive in a more fundamental life-or-death way than we do today. And back then, going off to find a new tribe was next to impossible.

So, while today it may seem like a child is being wildly dramatic with their demands for the shoes or hairstyle that will unite them with their group, what they are actually doing is precisely what their brain was designed to do. They are securing their position in the tribe so they don't get kicked out of the cave.

Naturally there are both good and bad ways this affects us, but understanding it is the first step to working with our brain in a healthy way. Remember, that F3 response can be used as jet fuel for your goal—all it needs is a target. When you open a door, your brain is happy to run through it. That's what our little three-letter word is. It's a doorway that directs all that F3 energy to develop ideas instead of sending it dashing down the street.

When you let your group's response stop you from trying new things, or limit yourself to only trying the things a miniature step away from what you already know how to do, that's when things go wrong. Before you know it, you start to see yourself as a different type of person. You've probably already guessed what type of person I mean.

You start to believe that you're the type of person who doesn't start anything unless you already know how to do it. You don't start unless you're already sure you're going to be good at it. It's a terrible mindset that narrows the scope of what you'll do in life. Not only that, it's just plain wrong. Because you're actually the type of person who figures things out. You always have been.

Here's what happened with Eric, the guy who really wanted to help me build a frame for a concrete countertop. He thought he was the type of person who couldn't start anything unless he knew how to do it. He couldn't get over the little voice in his head that said he might do something wrong, so he better not do anything at all. He let that voice get the best of him. He was so nervous about what it might feel like to do things wrong, that he did nothing.

Eric forgot something important about himself, though. He was actually the type of person who had figured out millions of things in his life. The fact that he had walked on his feet into my house proved that. But somewhere along the way, the terrible things happened and he pretended he wasn't that type of person anymore.

I knew it, though. And I also knew exactly what would have happened if Eric tried to build a frame for my concrete countertop.

He would have done it all wrong. I have no doubt about it. If he had randomly tried some stuff, he would have cut the wood too long or too short. He would have put something in the wrong place and we would have to take it out and do it over. He would have sucked at building a countertop frame because he had never done it before. He would have fallen flat on his face.

How am I so sure of that?

Because an hour after Eric went home, that's what I did. Because I didn't know how to do it either—yet. And just like the first time I walked across a room, I had to learn how everything coordinated together, build up my muscle and fall flat a few times before I got anywhere near something workable. Do you see what the biggest difference was between this guy Eric and me?

It wasn't skill. We were pretty equally skilled—or

unskilled—at framing this thing. It wasn't our desire to build it, we were equal there too. We had the same resources, tools, and materials. The only difference was that one little three-letter word. We both didn't know how to build it. But I approached it with the mindset that I didn't know how to build it *yet*.

Pass me a two-by-four. I'll just keep trying until I have something that works. Even if that means I do it wrong—probably a couple of times. Even if I fall on my face. Even if someone laughs at me. Because at the end of the day, I'll have built a countertop, a wall, a roof, even an entire house. And then, I'll be the one laughing.

Each Attempt Hones Your Skill

Ready to put this into action? Let's skip to the good part.

This little special effect isn't some kind of vague metaphor you have to construct from new ideas and learn how to apply to something totally new in your life. It's a simple principle applied in exactly the same way you have already used it. Just like when you were little, the only thing you have to know going into any project is that you want to do it. Next, you immediately start and keep trying things until you figure it out.

This principle keeps building on itself.

Each of the skills you learn doing the current project will help you do some part of the next project. In retrospect, this means I did have a slight advantage over Eric. I had a lifetime of trying to do all kinds of crazy projects, of learning what works and what absolutely does not work. So even if the only frame I had ever built was a picture frame, some of those same principles would apply to my countertop frame.

Remember, you don't have to know how to do the whole thing in order to move one step forward.

Diving straight in will feel uncomfortable at first, but your confidence level builds with each success. Every time you figure out something, you believe more strongly that you're the type of person who can figure things out. The benefits keep building. No pun intended. (Well, maybe.)

Remember, when I started building a house, I didn't know how to use a nail gun, set a concrete foundation block, frame a window, install a sink, or build a rafter. I didn't know how to do a single one of those things — YET. But I knew a lot of the small skills that I could creatively put together to figure out how to do those things. Every single day, every single project my kids and I did on our construction site to build a house, we went in with this idea. I don't know how to do that thing yet—but give me a minute and I'll figure it out.

You probably guessed that also means the first couple of times you leap right into a project and try some things you won't have a great skill base, and you're going to fall down quite a few times. Don't worry. You'll build up your skills and exercise your creative muscles. You'll get really good at combining weird skills that didn't seem like they had anything at all to do with each other and using them to do something entirely new and amazing. What this means is, it gets easier and easier for us to figure out more and more complex things.

Does that mean my kids and I came to the construction

site with so many skills that we didn't fail? We didn't ever do it wrong? Of course not. We did it wrong a dozen times. We framed out a window. Cut it apart. Did it again. And again. We kept doing that until it was right. We never thought of it as failing, we just thought: I don't know how to do that—yet. The next window was easier. By the time we did all of the windows we really had it figured out. And those skills—All the little things we figured out framing windows— were all going to help us for the next part of the project.

Have you tried and failed? Fantastic. You're doing great.

Shrug it off like you did when you were a kid who bounced right off the ground for the next try at walking. Keep getting back up and keep trying until all the times you said, *yet* add up to: I already know how to do that. What's next?

We all talk about how quickly young kids learn and how many new skills they pack into a few short years. But the ability to do this doesn't vanish as we get older. The same fast rate of doing and learning and accomplishing things will happen to you right now. All you have to do is dust off that childhood mindset.

Get yourself back into the habit of starting big projects even when you have no idea how to do them. Do it exactly the way you used to. Figure it out, one step at a time.

Figure It Out

Let's watch the yet principle in action by looking closely at a small but feisty goal setter known as Grandma Moses. This woman seriously knew how to use the magic behind the yet principle. If you haven't heard of this amazing lady, she's an artist. And a pretty well-known one at that. You've almost definitely seen her work even if you didn't know her name.

Grandma Moses painted landscapes in bright primary colors with a simple, nostalgic, and almost whimsical style. All of her paintings are a lot of fun. She seems to have figured out how to paint optimism. In fact, she once said that she painted her daydreams, which may remind you of our chapter on visualization. Grandma Moses imagined a happy world, and then she painted it, and I like that a lot.

As it turned out, a whole lot of other people like it too. And you guessed it, they pay a lot of money to hang her daydreams on their wall.

Not only have some of these paintings sold for over a million dollars, her artwork has sold on somewhere around 50 million Christmas cards. Not bad, right? Well, that's not even the impressive part of her story.

Let me tell you why she started to paint in the first place.

One of the most unusual things about Grandma Moses and her wild success, is that she never studied art. You heard me right, her paintings have sold for over a million dollars, over fifty million Christmas cards, celebrities have her art in their homes, but she didn't study art. Not only that, but she didn't even work at it for very long.

She actually spent a lot of time raising kids, taking care of her house, doing needlepoint, and some quilting, too. And she was pretty happy with all of this. Until one day, something terrible happened to her.

Grandma Moses developed such painful arthritis that

she couldn't do any kind of needle work. Don't get the mistaken idea here that this was a case of early-onset arthritis or anything, she was 78 years old. Seventy-eight, and looking for a new goal.

She tried to just sit still, enjoy what she had achieved in life. Feel content. But it didn't work. She couldn't shake that restless feeling that she could do more than she was doing. But then whenever she opened her sewing box and picked up a needle, she couldn't do what she loved. She felt stuck.

Picture it now, this 78-year-old woman was looking for something new to do with her time and talent. She had a very limited skill set so anything she tried to do would be brand new. It would be something she had no idea how to do—yet.

Thankfully Netflix wasn't around yet, because this was 1939. And without the option to pull out an iPad to play Candy Crush or solitaire, Grandma Moses' sister suggested she ought to try painting. After all, she had painted a little scene years before when she was wallpapering her parlor and ran out of wallpaper. That time she had used house paint to fill the empty spot with a lovely landscape painting of trees and a little pond.

She hadn't painted anything before or after that landscape, but now that she couldn't do her needlework, she wondered if she could make anything worthwhile. She thought of a happy little scene in her head, and then she immediately picked up a paint brush and painted. Naturally, she was a little nervous over how it would turn out. She had the same F3 response to doing things outside her comfort zone as you and I do. But she pointed that surge of energy straight at her empty piece of paper. Instead of dashing down the street, she let that little idea light up in her brain, and then she kept feeding the fire.

She painted happy farm scenes, holidays, and snow days. Simple realism in bright colors. They made her smile, so she kept going. When the finished art started piling up, she found a little drug store in town willing to sell her work. She just kept painting and selling and painting and selling.

Until one day in 1938 Louis Caldor, an art collector who was in Hoosick Falls, New York on vacation, bought some of Grandma Moses paintings from that drug store. The next day, he bought all the paintings she had on her farm. By 1939, her paintings had been in a show at New York's Museum of Modern Art. And the next year, when she was eighty years old, she had her first one-woman show at a New York Gallery.

She won awards, appeared on television and wrote an autobiography. Norman Rockwell even painted her into one of his paintings. Still, there she was, little old Grandma Moses painting and selling and painting. Until something terrible happened. Again.

It was the arthritis again. Her right hand hurt too much to hold the paintbrush. She was frustrated. She hated sitting still when she knew she could do so much more. She felt stuck—but not for long.

Because if anyone knew how to charge forward and try something new without pause, it was Grandma Moses. She had an idea. She fanned the flame. She fed the fire. She picked up the paintbrush with her left hand this time to attempt something she had no idea how to do yet.

She practiced until she could just pick right up where she'd left off, painting and selling.

Grandma Moses died in 1961 with around 1,500 paintings completed. She was 101.

Are you ready to pick up a paintbrush?

I'm kidding! Well, kind of.

Let's think this through a second. When I built a house, wrote a book, or started a speaking career, when Grandma Moses started painting, first with her right hand, then with her left, it was at a turning point, the cusp of change. It's not always exactly like that. It can be that everything in your life is just chugging along as usual but one day it's not enough anymore. One day, you feel restless and stuck. You've reached a turning point. And here's why I think that's really interesting.

You have to be a little dissatisfied with your life in order to change it. You have to not like something about it in order to reach for something bigger. You have to really want something. You realize on some level that there's a disconnect or a gap between where you are right now and what you're capable of.

You recognize your potential.

It all starts with a little feeling that you're stuck and you want to get unstuck.

The moment when you feel that, every single time you feel it in life, it has the potential to launch you toward a much better version of your life. Use those moments. Turn off Netflix and pick up a paintbrush. Start asking yourself lots of questions about what you want your future to look like.

What are some things you were interested in as a child

that you always thought you'd try someday? Start somewhere. That's all it takes.

Find a thing you don't know how to do yet, and figure it out.

CHAPTER NINE

The Last Person On Earth

THERE'S A WAY TO DO IT BETTER—FIND IT.
- THOMAS EDISON

I'm a sucker for a good survival story, so I was beyond excited in eighth grade when my English teacher passed out a novel about a bunch of kids stranded on an island. My brother and I had watched each *Gilligan's Island* episode about a thousand times, so I was pretty sure I knew exactly how this story was going to go. It turns out, I've never been more wrong in my life.

This story wasn't about the professor making a bamboo Geiger counter or Mary Ann running out of coconuts for her pie. No, this novel was called *Lord of the Flies*. Which, in case you missed reading it in school, is a much darker tale that kept me and generations of junior high school kids up at night.

Lord of the Flies was written in 1954 and it's about a group of six twelve-year-old boys who were stranded alone on an island. The boys establish a leader of sorts, but still descend quickly into all kinds of primitive, cruel behavior. They act a lot more like animals than boys from high class families. It was the last thing I was expecting, and it horrified me.

My general takeaway was that the same thing would happen to me and my classmates if the rule keepers of society disappeared. Just like these British school boys, we were all just one small step away from total chaos. The veneer of society suddenly felt very thin, which was a deep thought for me at the time. But honestly, that's not even what bothered me most about that book.

I hated the fall into madness for sure, but what was missing from this story were the things I loved most about survival stories. I had always been fascinated by all the innovative things that people in a survival situation might create to help them survive and even thrive. Those details were the best part of all the survival stories I'd ever heard. The idea that people could create some kind of tool from an unexpected item, or use an old thing in a brand-new way. That "a-ha" moment over everyday tasks that would be so simple if only you had a book of matches, a sewing kit, or a toolbox absolutely thrilled me. This book was missing the coconut shell drum set and the bamboo bicycle-driven washing machine, and I felt cheated.

If my brother and I were stranded on an island, I was positive we would have valued creative survival and having fun over a jungle-like power struggle. And when I looked around at my classmates, I thought it was true for them too.

Let's get to the burning question that I know has you on the edge of your seats. Which model was right? Did that fictional *Lord of the Flies* novel know something innate about human nature that I was too young to see? Or was I right that my classmates would help me create a bamboo plumbing system and a beach badminton court?

I recently found the answer in a real-life story about six boys who were stranded on an island alone for 15 months. Their story is like something straight from Hollywood, and you're going to love it.

But first, I want to show you why this matters. This survival instinct is important because all of us feel that same thrill in those "a-ha" moments, and that feeling is one of the best tools to get us unstuck. Want to know what we can do with that?

Here's the real gold. We can set this up on purpose any time we're faced with a step and have absolutely no idea how to begin.

You've already gone through your setup visualization and you're ready to take a quick first action step, you've even run through the worst case scenario and yet principle. But none of this is working because those tricks don't make up for the fact that you still don't know how to do the thing in front of you.

Do you want to know how I get past that moment?

I use a special survival-inspired special effect when my mind needs a jolt of creative energy, it's one that helps me see old tools in a new way and creatively figure out an unexpected way to take that step. I call this my last person on earth scenario, and it's incredibly effective.

Not only does this trick take advantage of the way our brains already work, it also mirrors the way how-to videos elevate the stakes to get our mind moving.

Survival Mindset Cheat

I promise we'll get to the story about the boys on the island, but let's look at a really simple application of this strategy first by using one of the ways I got my kids moving when they were stuck on a sticky step—literally.

My kids full-out panicked when they were faced with exceptionally difficult tasks that would have a huge life-long impact. Things like spreading peanut butter on a soft piece of bread all by themselves for the first time. We've all seen a similar thing play out with kids, even if it was mayo or—lord help us—globs of grape jelly. I've personally witnessed more than one kid seriously lose their mind over the idea of taking the first step on a sandwich project.

My oldest daughter Hope made an especially grand scene over this. Waving her hands wildly and explaining, (Read the following in a teary four-year-old voice for the best immersive experience.) "Mommy, I just can't! You're so much better at it than I am. You make it perfect. I know I complained about the edges before, but you make it perfect! The bread will definitely get ruined if I do it." Here she made a tiny tear in the bread and gasped to demonstrate how devastating this would be. She went on to tell me, "There will be peanut butter everywhere if I try and you know you won't like that."

You get the idea. This went on long enough for the bread to go a little stale.

It's a low-stakes problem to the adult, and a life altering survival-level problem to the kid. So rather than argue with Hope's brain on this one, which we all know is a waste of time with any kid, I played right into the level of drama her brain was dishing out. What I'm saying is, I pulled out my last person on earth strategy.

Let me warn you right from the start that the following strategy may fall under the if-you-can't-beat-em-join-em strategy. But I'm cool with that because it works.

I said to Hope, "If you were the last person on earth, and you had to spread peanut butter on your bread in order to live, could you do it?"

Of course she could.

One corner of her mouth curled up in a determined little smirk. And then she did it. She spread the peanut butter on the bread. You can be sure she used methods I'd never thought of. She tried curving the slice of bread and putting it directly into the jar to wipe the peanut butter on it. No good. She tried using a spoon instead of a butter knife but it was no good either. She plopped some peanut butter on her plate and flipped it upside down onto the bread—which didn't work at all but gave her another idea. And then another.

It was an absolute disaster of a sandwich. Thick globs bulged in some spaces and the bread was clean as a whistle in others. Both sides of each slice were sticky. The bread had holes and tears. The counter had three times more peanut butter than the bread, and there were also generous amounts on Hope's left foot. But somehow my picky girl didn't care all that much. What she held in her sticky fingers was no longer just a sandwich. This was the sandwich she had made to save her life.

At first glance this is a silly example, but it's important because it scales up to every single situation where you don't have a single idea how to begin. The last person on earth sandwich is the answer you've been looking for. I know you're thinking I'm as nutty as Hope's peanut butter right now, and that's okay. After we take a closer look at why this works, you'll be on team sandwich. Ready to dig in?

Let's stick with the peanut butter sandwich for a quick analysis and move up to life-and-death situations in just a minute—because Mama says bite-sized pieces are easiest to digest.

When Hope first faced off against her sandwich, she imagined making it using only the skills she already had. And she knew herself pretty well. She'd been frustrated with the way her Play-Doh creations or finger paintings never turned out exactly the way she pictured them in her head. She knew her coordination was still under development and her butter knife skills were lacking. She also had a high expectation of the finished product based on her experience of a skilled person (that was me) with countless hours of butter knife practice doing the labor.

Every single time Hope imagined her sandwich project, it traveled through the same paths in her brain and landed in the same place. Which we can assume was a trash bin overflowing with unacceptable sandwiches.

My simple question did something really unique.

"If you were the last person on earth and you had to do this to live, could you do it?"

First, it jolted the sandwich project to a completely different path. Suddenly it was the last person on earth sandwich, and that changed everything. On this path, there were fewer rules and expectations. All the usual excuses and limitations she imagined were instantly broken, especially the limits that come from other people's opinions. Because, after all, she was the only person left on earth.

This is a scenario that shifts not just a single idea, like the yet principle and worst case scenario effects do, but this is a powerhouse of a game changer because it widens the possibilities in every direction. When the boundaries expand three dimensionally like this, anything is possible.

The second thing my survival question gave her was a brand-new storyline to follow in her head. Sure, it was a little bit ridiculous, but that's actually why she paid attention to it. This ridiculous image of her as the last girl on earth who for some unknown reason must spread peanut butter on bread to survive was captivating. That silly, playful image woke up the creative part of her brain. Suddenly, she could be more innovative because instead of following an established path that led directly to the sandwich trash bin, she had a little fire burning in her mind that would warm up the surrounding pathways until she had more and more ideas of how to accomplish her task.

A huge part of what motivates us to do anything is the story we tell ourselves in our head. When you mix it up with a huge departure from your usual story, you wake up your creative mind and can get some really amazing results. You see old things in a brand-new way, which happens to be the key to beginning hard things.

A similar version of this played out with Drew when he was about 13 and I asked him to open the dreaded pickle jar. He tried, said he couldn't, and handed it back to me. And I replied, "If we can't open that jar, you have to return it to the store with me and tell them we can't have the pickles because we can't open the jar." We both laughed over that scenario. It was wacky. It was embarrassing. But if we really couldn't open the pickles, it was also a real possible solution.

No one stronger than Drew or me was going to magically show up and open the jar. If we wanted pickles, we had to figure out how to open the jar. So, I said, "We're the last people on earth Drew, and we have to open the pickles to live, what are we trying next?"

We tried every stuck-lid trick known to mankind, and we got it unstuck. Because that's what this special effect does. It loosens the rules and wakes up that creative part of your brain to get you unstuck.

Pro pickle jar tip: Poke a hole in the lid with a nail to loosen a sealed lid. And the only reason we were willing to try this is because under our survival scenario it no longer mattered if we ruined a perfectly good jar lid. The boundaries had expanded and the only important thing was getting to the pickles.

You Are Innately Creative

I promised you a true-life story of shipwreck and survival to go along with this effect, and you're going to love it. Unlike the plane crash that stranded the fictional characters in *Lord of the Flies*, this true story starts in 1965 with six boys between 13 and 16 years of age who skipped school and set off on an adventure. They had the wild idea that they would all sail up to Fiji together for a little vacation.

The fact that Fiji was nearly 500 miles away didn't slow them down at all. Neither did that fact that they didn't own a boat, or that they lived in the most populated city in the Tongan kingdom and only had a few basic boating skills between them. They spotted a small, unattended sailboat they thought would do the trick, and they swiped it without permission.

Since the list of things they didn't have is longer than the list of things they did, let's talk about that. They didn't have an engine on that boat, or a map or compass, they also didn't have much food or water, only some bananas and coconuts. They also had a gas burner because they imagined they could just catch and eat fish on their 500-mile trip. They didn't have survival skills any greater than you or I did at their age, and they certainly didn't have the ability to navigate a small boat for hundreds of miles in the open ocean. It's probably no surprise to you that this trip took a bad turn.

The first night, a storm ripped off their sails and broke their rudder, which means the six boys were just drifting aimlessly, pretty sure they were going to die.

They drifted for eight days before they saw a volcanic island and briefly thought it was a miracle. But then they realized that in order to get ashore they would have to smash their boat against the jagged shoreline. With no other options, they smashed into the small uninhabited speck-on-the map island and somehow all managed to get to shore alive. A feat that was impossible to celebrate when they were starving, dehydrated, and hundreds of miles from the route they'd planned.

In that moment, these boys landed smack in a scenario that jolts our brains into creative solution mode. They were living my question in real time.

"If you were the last person on earth and you had to do this to live, could you do it?"

It turns out, they could.

They were forced to look at the core of themselves and discover what they were made of. How deep could you dig in this scenario?

Those boys had none of the tools or conveniences they were used to. But they also had none of the boundaries or rules. How they survived or even if they did was totally up to them. There's nothing like this kind of a life-or-death scenario to light some creative fires in your brain.

Imagine how strong their F3 response was pumping. They had a pile of new ideas, and the energy to execute them. And boy were they going to need it.

One of the most important features this mindset brings to the table is urgency. Without having to even think about it, you get a built-in deadline. This was even true in our pickle jar scenario, which could honestly have been shelved. There was no real urgency for us to have pickles, but we felt like there was the second we framed it with the last person on earth scenario. A deadline may seem like a small and unimportant thing, but it isn't. It's actually an indicator of success.

You're not only more likely to hit a goal that has a deadline, the tighter your deadline is, the greater your odds of hitting it. The challenge and urgency of a deadline amps up the number of resources your brain is willing to allocate to the task. So, by intentionally moving tasks into this high stakes mode, we are more likely to figure out how to execute them and also to do this quickly.

That's a recipe for success when you're faced with something you have no idea how to do. Like how to survive on a deserted island with no food, water, or supplies.

Let's get back to our regularly scheduled program.

The schoolboys were thirsty and hungry, and solving those needs was a life-or-death project. Could they figure out how to get some food? Of course they could. First, they scavenged every piece of their smashed boat, imagining how they might use each scrap in brand new ways. When they found an oar and a piece of wire, they turned it into a pole and caught their first meal in eight days. They ate the fish raw, and then began looking for other sources of food and water.

Eventually they discovered an area where sea birds nested and were able to eat the raw eggs, and also the raw birds. It was dangerous to chase the birds on the steep cliff where they nested though and at one point one of the boys fell and broke his leg. They weren't sure how to help him, but there they were the last people on earth and they would have to do this to survive, and so they did. The boy's leg took months to heal in a makeshift splint, but eventually he could use it as well as he had before the break.

It took them six months to finally learn to light a fire by

rubbing sticks together, and then they had to protect that fire endlessly from that moment on, even building a shelter around it to guard it from the rain and wind.

Unlike the boys in *Lord of the Flies*, these boys created systems that worked to not only survive, but to thrive on the island together. The oldest two became the leaders, one for instruction and guidance and the other for care and emotional support. Occasionally they argued and were frustrated with each other, like when they were struggling to build a hut, or hunting for enough sea birds to feed everyone—two birds each day. But when they argued, they agreed to take a walk in opposite directions in the jungle to calm down. Then they returned to solve the problem.

Eventually, they found the ruins of an old village that was raided by slave traders hundreds of years before they arrived. There, they found the descendants of chickens, and enough vegetable plants to begin a garden. They planted beans, yucca, bananas, and eventually had a flock of 200 chickens. Having a stock of eggs on hand changed everything, and when the weather made it too dangerous to hunt sea birds, they would eat a chicken.

It was hard work feeding scraps of coconut to the chickens, tending the fire and the garden, and getting fresh water. But their minds had plenty of creative energy left over for fun too. They played badminton, exercised, and even made a guitar out of wood scraps, a coconut, and some wire scraps. They wrote songs and sang together. And they still have this guitar today.

After being stranded on the island for fifteen months— they counted the days on a slate and later learned they were only off by two days—the boys had accepted that they might never be rescued, but they hadn't given up hope entirely. They took turns at a lookout post at a highpoint on the island. Four different times they spotted a ship and ran to start huge fires, but each time the ship sailed away without noticing their signal. Until one day a captain noticed the black scorch marks on the island and heard faint calls that sounded as much like birds as they did like boys, and this time, the ship sailed in for a closer look.

The captain's name was Peter Warner, and when six naked boys with wild hair that hadn't been cut in 15 months swam up to his boat with an incredible story, he didn't believe it was true. In fact, he thought they might be escaped convicts. Finally, they convinced him to call a radio operator back home who said it was true and that the boys had been given up for dead.

Can you imagine what it was like the moment Warner docked in the very place the boys had started their adventure almost a year and a half earlier?

Well, because nothing in life goes the way you expect, you probably imagined it all wrong. What actually happened is that the man whose boat they stole pressed charges and the boys were all arrested. That's when Warner saved them a second time by promising to help raise the money to pay for the ruined boat by filming a documentary about the boys.

Finally, they were released to go home where they came ashore to the days and days of feasting that you'd imagine for six boys who set off on an adventure and instead landed in a real-life deserted island scenario.

I love this story for the creativity and determination of

those boys. I love it even more because I know you and I have this same ability to come up with extraordinary solutions to take on any task. And best of all, I love this proof that we can throw our brain into a version of this hyper creative mode simply by asking ourselves a single question.

"If you were the last person on earth and you had to do this to live, could you do it?"

Your brain will pull up surges of energy, enthusiasm, creativity and bold ideas you never imagined you were capable of. We're talking lift-a-car-off-an-injured-stranger level of energy and Isaac Newton level brainstorms. When you frame any situation as a survival situation, you tap into some serious power.

Elevate the Urgency

This special effect works. The results will surprise you because the ideas your mind tosses out will be radically different from anything you would normally try—but that's actually the point. You've already set your project up to align perfectly with how-to video strategy. You've added the word yet to the end of your uncertainty. You've calculated the worst case scenario and know that the risk is no big deal compared to your reward. When you've done all of this but you still can't think of a way to begin the first step, then you need something radical to get you moving.

Try one small idea. Try it quickly, and then try one more.

To get a better handle on how this works, let's look at the equivalent in a how-to video. Have you ever been decorating for a holiday and the video host practically screams at you, "Grab your hot glue gun like you're the last person on earth and you have to get this glitter garland right in order to survive!"

No? Me either.

I'm guessing that even if you've watched hundreds of tutorials, you've never heard anything close to this. Because it's just too ridiculous for that direct of an approach. A statement like that would have to come with an explanation, and by design these videos steer clear of lengthy explanations in order to keep us focused and moving forward with the first step and every step after that.

If they don't use the last person on earth question, then how does a tutorial video use this strategy? It's actually really obvious once you know what to look for.

When we look closely at this effect, what it's really doing is raising the urgency of a task while adding fun and a challenge.

Let's break that down using an example we're pretty familiar with by now, Mac and the how to drive a car video he watched before heading to McDonalds for a cheeseburger.

At first glance, there was nothing urgent about in the video as we imagined it. But two things build urgency into a tutorial. The first is the clear set up step where we can visualize that end goal in a perfect, larger than life view of what it's going to look like when we have it. For Mac, this was the way he saw himself driving to get the goods for himself and his little sister. When a video really sets this up clearly enough for us to want it badly, we feel an urgency to have it.

The second move a video brings to the table to set this

up in our mind as an urgent task is the speed that it moves from one step to the next. We already talked about how that speed sneaks past our excuses, but this is an even closer look at how slipping the actions in quickly motivates us into action. Our brain equates speed with urgency.

Think about the last time you were rushing around doing something and someone said, "Whoa, whoa, what's the emergency?"

Maybe you were doing a task you don't like and just trying to get it over with. Or maybe you had plans and were trying to fit in a pile of things before you had to leave the house. Even though there was no true emergency, your brain elevated the status and even convinced your body to expend some extra energy to get that task done.

No matter how a task gets elevated to hyper-speed mode, our brain elevates the urgency.

In Mac's case, he brought a little urgency of his own to the table in the form of a growling tummy. He was hungry, not in a general way, but specifically hungry for a McDonalds cheeseburger. His sister was hungry too, and in the way of small children everywhere, I'm willing to bet she asked him somewhere between three and three hundred times, "Are you ready, Mac? Can we leave now? What about now? Are we going?"

Urgent tasks get special treatment in our mind and body. Urgent tasks get us moving.

The other two things a how-to video does that create the same thing as our last person on earth question, is that they create challenge and fun. I already mentioned the deadline, which is one of the most important ways our mind is challenged by a project, but there are other ways that a new project challenges us, too. Just the idea of doing something new stimulates our brain, and so does the idea that we can later show someone else what an amazing new thing we've achieved. That's why videos often have an audience element.

In the driving video, that end goal didn't show a person driving across a farmer's field. It was the public nature of driving down a public road and waiving at smiling people that challenged Mac to show off a little bit.

Think back to my lemon cake, which one would assume I didn't intend to eat alone. The challenge of having a new skill to put on display is as attractive to our mind as learning to fish with an oar and a piece of wire was to the schoolboys on that island. Sure, the stakes were much higher for the boys, but the challenge is alive in both cases.

I'm Here For the Storytelling

Finally, let's talk about fun—an essential element in every project—and we'll actually give it a little more attention in another chapter. You probably don't immediately think of fun when I say, "Imagine you're the last person on earth." But our minds love nothing more than a good story. Sometimes our own day-to-day story starts to feel stale. Our brain gets tired of going down the same paths over and over again. We get hungry for something new.

A tutorial video not only gives us a new storyline for our task, but it also adds elements of special effects fun.

Was the idea of driving to McDonalds on his own fun for Mac? You bet! And that driving video made it even more fun with sound effects, jokes, slow-mo, time lapse, and maybe even some cartoon animations. It took a potentially scary new task and lowered the risk by making it feel more fun than scary.

When you introduce this last person on earth story, your brain leaps into that new character role with a little grin, ready to accept the challenge. You've introduced a kind of a game in the middle of a time where you were struggling with something difficult, and that shift changes everything.

If this sounds a little bit like a magic trick, that's because it is. It's a little slight-of-hand trick to reroute your problem for elevated performance. But like all magic tricks, it'll get old if you keep showing the same trick over and over again.

This trick in particular is one to save for the really stuck moments.

There's a good reason I didn't start our special effect section with the last person on earth scenario. For one, you understand it a lot better because you now understand many of the principles behind how your brain processes information and action and how you can use that to your advantage. But more importantly, I saved this effect because you should try the other ones first. Why do I say this?

Because constantly tossing your brain into urgent mode will just plain make you tired. Sending your mind to the most creative reaches to figure things out burns a ton of resources. Sometimes you need that level of brain power to figure out how in the world to begin the thing in front of you. That's how humans get themselves out of the tough spots.

But sometimes you can quickly get moving by going through our model. You can take an easy first step, or remind yourself that the worst case scenario is totally survivable, or that you don't have to know how to do the whole project in order to do the step directly in front of you.

Can you see how all of these things work together?

I don't just mean all the effects of this last person on earth scenario. I mean all the things we've talked about from the first sentence of this book until now. We're not talking about a bunch of random disconnected things you might try when you're stuck, we're looking at a connected system of mind and body that's based on the way your automatic internal systems already work.

We've identified how a tutorial video takes advantage of your built-in systems to get you up and moving, and we're learning how you can set your own goals up to take advantage of those same systems.

Now can you see why I was so excited about discovering the press play effect?

Of course you can.

Before we call this a wrap, I have one more special effect to share with you. In the way of a grand finale, I've saved one of my favorite tricks for last.

CHAPTER TEN

The Quit Early Effect

AN ANT ON THE MOVE DOES MORE THAN A DOZING OX. - LAO TZU

If you were stranded on an island today, no one would have to remind you that to stay alive you would have to spend a lot of time every day hunting and gathering food. Eating would be on your mind from the time you stepped out of your beach hut every morning until you fell asleep to the waves lapping at your private beach each night. You would never lose your motivation to wake up and get food, because you would feel hungry.

One of the best ways to stay motivated for any goal is to stay hungry.

Now that you know how to set up your goal with strong visualization, you can start out as hungry for your goal as

Mac was for his MacDonald's cheeseburger. You also know how to take a quick first step which gives you even more ownership of the goal and keeps you hungry. But even with these how-to video tools in your belt, we all know some projects need a little extra motivation.

Sometimes as the work gets more difficult, your motivation fades away. That's when the end starts to look impossibly far away. Every step feels as difficult to start as the first step, and the only thing you're really hungry for is quitting time.

Building a house was like that for me sometimes. It wasn't just hard to talk myself into doing that work on the first day we broke ground. It kept being hard. When my entire body was covered with bruises and every muscle ached and all the things that could have gone wrong that day had gone wrong in the worst way, what I wanted most was an exit strategy.

The morning after a day like that, I had to talk myself into stepping back on that construction site all over again. With zero idea how to frame a window or run gas lines, that was a tough morning conversation with my mirror. I could think of a whole pile of excuses to not show up that day, and for a while this kept happening. Until one day I figured out how to apply a special effect that pulled me back out to our muddy site day after day. In fact, once I figured out how to do this one small thing, nothing could have kept us away.

The trick was to make that first step of the day feel like a continuation from the day before instead of like a brand-new step. That's right, it's not a first step if it's a second step.

I found this amazing motivation solution in the most

unlikely place. And even though it will put my strange reading habits on blast, I want to share my entire journey down this path because the discovery of this process in its full bizarre form is both part of the fun and part of the success.

We Remember Interrupted Tasks

You know how this sort of thing begins. I was reading about how to secure a wall's bottom plate to concrete when I clicked on a thing that led me to a thing, and the next thing I knew I was reading about a Russian psychologist in the 1930s. Minutes later I was elbow deep in an article about game theory and an addictive little puzzle game called Tetris. Remember that one? I first saw it on a Nintendo GameBoy, and it's seductively simple. Differently shaped blocks fall from the sky and you rotate them so they will fall into exactly the right place. It's an easy, repetitive game. And I already know what you're thinking.

What in the world do a Russian psychologist and a puzzle game that wasted a lot of time in the early '90s have in common? It just so happens they share a lot more than the fact that the annoying digitized Tetris tune that burrowed into our brain was a loop of Russian folk music. Ready for the big (weird) reveal?

These two very different things focused on the exact same behavior in our brains. It's an automatic thing that works the same way for every one of us. You know me well enough by now to know that's my kind of thing. A thing like that might send me down an all-night reading rabbit hole—which is exactly what happened.

And what I found down that rabbit hole was an unlikely solution to get me up and moving on all the frustrating first steps in my house building project and every project after that. All I had to do was make my project feel as addictive as a Tetris game and my problem was solved.

Sound impossible? It isn't.

The Russian psychologist I read about was a woman named Bluma Zeigarnik. Back in the early 1930s, she was hanging out in a busy cafe and doing what psychologists do best—people watching. When it was her turn to place an order, she was stunned by how perfectly the waiter remembered every detail of her order and also each order at the nearby tables without a notepad or recorder. You've seen this party trick too, right? The waiter nods at the most complicated order and lands every item perfectly for a party of twelve. It's impressive.

Oddly enough, Zeigarnik didn't actually care at all that they remembered the details, what she noticed was how long they remembered them. It turned out, the moment the orders were delivered to the table, the waiter forgot them completely. Weird, right?

The order stuck tight in their brain only until the food hit the table in front of the hungry patron. Then, poof! Vapor. The waiter walked away and instantly had no idea who had the stroganoff with a beer and who had the borsht with a side salad. Zeigarnik knew this was more than bizarre, it was a little window into how our brains manage tasks. She immediately set up a study to test this.

The memory theory she developed not only holds up today, it's become the foundation of many new memory theories. What she discovered is that interrupted tasks stick in our memory. A simple but profound truth. Unfinished things hold a special place in our brain, but once they're completed? Poof! Vapor. This may seem boring on its own but stay with me because this is where the idea turns into something really cool.

One of Zeigarnik's colleagues, a Russian psychologist named Maria Ovsiankina, said what you probably just said, "Well, so what?" She didn't think the discovery was completely irrelevant, because it did mean that her coffee and eggs arrived as requested every day. But she also believed this idea needed to be followed a little further to be useful. And I happen to agree with her.

Ovsiankina uncovered an even more interesting application for this theory—at least for our purposes. She discovered that when a task is interrupted before it's finished, we don't just remember it, we almost always go back and finish it.

Let that sink in.

It's a subtle addition, but it's so important. Especially when you apply it to things outside of that little cafe, like your very important projects. If you stop a task before it's finished, you feel an irresistible urge to go back and finish it. What's that? An irresistible urge to go do your work? Now that's something we could all use in our lives. Because it sounds (and is) exactly like a built-in motivation factory.

If you stop before something's finished, you're going to go back and finish it. We're not talking about a small likelihood here. According to this principle, you are 90 percent more likely to finish any task that you stop just before you reach the end. That's huge. It not only changes your chances of success; It changes how you can set up that success right from the first step.

The Last Piece is the Best Piece

I know you have more than one unfinished project laying around, so I feel you pulling out the uh-uhs right now. Relax while I add one all-important detail: How and where you interrupted the project is critical to create the irresistible tug back to finish it. That means what we're really learning here is exactly where to set our quitting time each day.

Let's lay out a simple example before we talk about why this works and how we can use it.

Imagine your best friend drops off a huge jigsaw puzzle just before you are snowed in by yourself for a week. Each day you spend a few hours working on this puzzle. It's a massive beast with 5,000 pieces. The sheer size of it is overwhelming at first.

Some days you even look for excuses not to work on it because it feels impossible. But you keep going back a little at a time until finally by the end of the week you can see you'll finally finish this puzzle. That day it's a little easier to get going and maybe you work longer than usual. You want to finish this thing. By the time sun sets and your back feels stiff from leaning over the table, you're nearly finished. You're so close you can taste this puzzle victory.

Only five pieces left! Then four, three, two…

You scurry around, looking everywhere for the final piece, but it's missing. A single hole gapes just left of the center in this massive puzzle. You shake the box. You crawl around under the table and move your chair. You shake your clothes to see if somehow that piece slipped up your sleeve. You check under your water glass. Nope. It's just not there.

Finally, you call the friend who dropped the puzzle off. She goes to her puzzle closet, and sure enough, there's one lone piece sitting on the shelf. The roads will be clear in the morning and she'll bring it by.

You watch some television. Read a book. But that puzzle with the one missing piece is still on your mind. It's not like you've really been robbed of anything. You can see on the cover of the box what that finished puzzle will look like. There's no mystery here. But still, leaving that one piece undone sticks in your mind. You didn't feel this way on all the other nights after you called quitting time on the puzzle. This feeling is unique. It happens when you quit very close to the end. Your project was interrupted at exactly the right moment to create an irresistible tug back to finish it. This is a perfect example of how the Ovsiankina effect pulls you back to finish what you started.

Here's how this scenario plays out. The next morning as soon as you get breakfast on the table, your friend knocks on the door and hands you that final piece. What will you do?

Will you eat breakfast and maybe go for a walk before you put that last piece in place? Maybe watch TV and check your email?

No. Way.

You rush to that puzzle before your first sip of coffee. And as you finally press that final piece neatly into place, you feel a rush of satisfaction. It's an actual physical response.

You sigh. Your shoulders drop. You take a deep breath and smile. It's not just a relief, it's a boost. You feel better in every way and happier in general. You even have more energy and feel more optimistic. It feels really great to complete things like this puzzle. But why? Why did you feel that irresistible pull to go back to that puzzle? And can we possibly make your projects as irresistible as that final puzzle piece?

Yes, we can. And this priceless trick isn't even difficult. Let's start with an explanation of the thing inside us that creates the irresistible pull.

One of the reasons we go back and finish what we started is because of how our brain rewards us at the finish line. Our brain sends out a burst of a feel-good chemical called dopamine. I'm not going to go into a full brain study here, but I do want to run through some simple facts so you understand enough to easily harness this little chemical for your own use.

Simply put, dopamine is the chemical that makes you feel good when you finish something. And it also creates a little pocket of memory that says, when you finish a thing like this you feel great because of it. That memory will strongly urge you to do that thing again so you can get the reward again. This is how habits form—both the good ones and the bad ones. Because memory doesn't just store each action all by itself, it stores these more like a movie scene: First this happens, and because of that this, until finally a happy ending where dopamine makes you feel great.

Dopamine does a lot more than just make you happy, though—it also gives you a burst of energy, helps you focus, remember, and learn. You put the last piece of the puzzle in, and the tree-like neuropathways in your brain flare up like someone sprayed gasoline on them.

That's not what you'd expect at all, is it? When you FINISH something, you'd expect except the fire to just fizzle out to ash. But instead, you get a flash of hot, feel-good fire that not only wraps up your project—get ready for the good part—it also sparks a new fire nearby.

What this means is that if you time the end of one step well, it will naturally and automatically set off the next fire, and therefore the next step of your project. Ending one step launches the next. You know what happens when you use this?

You create an unbreakable motivation chain.

How? You quit early.

But let me warn you, that doesn't mean what you think it means.

Quit Before the End

The quit early effect doesn't mean knocking off work at three o'clock so you can grab a beer or hit the gym. It's a brain engaging strategy where instead of wrapping things up neatly before your lunch break or at the end of the day, you leave a final step undone. You leave the last puzzle piece right there on the table, and you walk away.

I know that it sounds too simple to be effective. But it works, and you'll get a feel for why as I go through a few examples. Remember, your brain, my brain, and all human brains work exactly the same way when it comes to feeling a pull back to an interrupted task. That means this quit early strategy will work for all of us. Let's set up a couple examples to see this effect in action.

Tetris is a good place to begin. And not just Tetris, but a zillion other video games like Bejeweled, Candy Crush, and countless popular games that hack into this loop of our brain's dopamine rewards. Not into video games? You haven't escaped this brain hacking. Jigsaw puzzles, billiards, checkers, and even eating junk food all tap into this same reward system.

Here's how this works. These games appeal to our brain's desire for order. We all prefer order and patterns, and this is true whether your house is neat-freak perfect right now or a little touch of chaos. Most games give us a simple scenario of a mess that we can easily clean up. And because we have a memory pocket that clearly says, *when you clean up a mess, you get a dopamine reward*, we are drawn to these games to clean up the messes over and over again.

Maybe the mess is made of jewels that you can easily line up into a row with a simple finger swipe, or a falling puzzle piece you turn just the right way, or a messy pool table that you can systematically clean up by shooting each ball into a pocket.

See the similarity between these games now? They may look nothing alike on the surface, but they all access the same reward system in your brain.

Each time you successfully clean or organize the game board in front of you, a burst of dopamine is released and you feel great about your achievement. With a game like pool or a jigsaw puzzle, you have a clear ending point, and while you may play a couple games in a row, you're probably not as addicted to these games as you are to Tetris. And that's because video games can more perfectly use the Zegarnik effect to endlessly interrupt your finish line.

Sure, you just dropped that piece in place and successfully blasted the whole row away, but a new mess is already falling from the sky. Problem, success, interruption, success, interruption, success, and all along you're getting rewarded by regular blasts of dopamine that keep you focused, concentrating, and commanding your brain to do this again and again and again.

It'll be no surprise to you at all that video sites like YouTube and TikTok use similar techniques to keep us watching video after video after video. Netflix uses it, too. The end of episode one drops a cliffhanger that is interrupted by the end credits. Do you want to stop there? No! Your brain says, if you just watch a bit more, I'll reward you for wrapping that story up nice and neat. Then that dopamine and the storyline warm the next storyline up, and they've successfully pulled you into a motivation chain, the one that keeps you binge-watching.

That's the press play effect in action, because it's our brain in action.

What an amazing, automatic system!

If, and only if, we use it for something a lot more productive than the next level of a game or the next episode or video. Which is exactly what you're here for.

The First Step is the Hardest

I couldn't believe my luck the moment I understood how all

of this worked. Because I knew if the how-to videos had figured out how to use this built-in system, then I could use it, too. This is how I did it.

I set up intentional interruptions for our jobs on the construction site. That's right, I interrupted our finish on purpose. I stopped the work before we reached the end so we'd be pulled back to do it, which set off a motivation chain reaction.

That, my friend, is what the quit early effect is all about.

I started using this trick at quitting time to guarantee I didn't have to argue myself back to work the next day. I would quit just short of actually finishing whatever I was working on. If I was laying a long row of concrete blocks, I'd leave the last one out. A gaping hole on top of our wall like a lost tooth. Picture that. It's maddening, isn't it? You get a little irritated feeling between your shoulder blades when you imagine it, a restless little wiggle to just wrap up that task before you leave. Why do we feel that way over a single block?

It's an interrupted task. And your brain doesn't like things to sit there nearly done, because it wants the burst of dopamine that will reward you if you just do that one last thing. I didn't give in, though. I would force myself to walk away from that gaping hole. Do you think I had to talk myself or the kids into getting back out to the site the next day after work and school?

No! We were practically running out there. We couldn't mix the mortar fast enough to get that last block in place on that row. And then, sigh; it was complete. That burst of "we did it" dopamine relaxed the restless wiggle and for just a minute we soaked that in. We high-fived each other and smiled. We felt capable and even a little invincible. Then that flare of chemical set off a spark that warmed up the nearby areas in our brains.

Not only did the quit early effect get us started each day or after lunch or dinner, it also gave us a head start of motivation on the next task. It was a seamless chain that kept us getting up and out to the site without fighting all the usual procrastination habits that make it hard to start a difficult next step. That first step of the next phase didn't feel like a daunting first step anymore because it was the second step of the day. We turned that first step into a second step. And we kept going. We started the next row of blocks or whatever was next on that day's to-do list.

Very cool, right?

We've all felt the pull to finish the last little part of some task before we put it on pause. This pull is so irresistible that we even announce it out loud. "Hold on," you say. "Just let me finish this one part." Because you want to get to a point that feels finished enough to give you that satisfaction. Ahhhh. That part is complete. Which feels great for the moment, but you're now a lot less likely to feel a desperate pull back to continue that project or task. Because once you hit a finish line, that task is literally moved out of your memory. Poof! Vapor. But if you instead interrupt it, that's like planting a little mental flag in your mind. "Don't you dare forget to come back and put that last piece in place ASAP!"

There are so many times I see evidence of this effect. Maybe you're reading and someone asks you a question, you hold up one finger and we all know what it means without a word. *Let me finish this paragraph and I'll be right with you.* Or your partner says, "It's time to go, I'll warm up the car" when you're almost done emptying the dishwasher.

Do you leave the last three clean plates in the dishwasher and leave? No, you say, "I'm almost done. I'll be out in a minute."

We do this even as very small children. And we get really frustrated when we aren't allowed to finish. Mom calls, "Come do your chores," but you feel a strong pull to finish the game you're playing or the page you're coloring, or the song you're listening too.

This is such a universal pull that we even have a well understood response when we feel this. "Hold on, I'm right in the middle of this _____" movie/book/game/call/project etc. When someone says this, we immediately understand how strong that person's brain is urging them not to quit in the middle. They are resisting the interruption.

We are hard-wired to finish things.

Our brains are made specifically to reward us for finishing things. And we can use this to our advantage. At the end of the day when you're about to quit and go home for a shower, resist the urge to wrap up the last steps of your task. As badly as you want that dopamine burst, it would be kind of wasted. Think about it, if you finish the task and get your reward—Poof!—it's over. There's nothing pulling you back. What a waste.

I mean it would feel good, sure. But imagine how much more useful it is if you can save it for the start of your next work day. The second you arrive on the construction site there's no uncertainty over what to do. You put that last block in place and immediately your brain and body get a boost that launches you straight ahead. Dopamine makes you happy and gives you more energy. It's a rush of brain power and it gives you a huge advantage.

Remember, according to Maria Ovsiankina, you are 90 percent more likely to finish any task that you stop just shy of the end. And by using the physical and mental boost from this effect as your quitting and starting point, you create a momentum cycle by making the first step of the day an easy one. The energy of one completed step then launches you into the next part of your goal.

Think of this as the cliff hanger at the end of a book chapter. Fiction writers in particular learn to never end a chapter with a satisfying conclusion. You never want to give a reader an obvious place to put a bookmark. Keep them turning pages. TV shows and even YouTube videos use the same principle with commercial breaks or an end-of-show cliffhanger. Soap operas are especially good at using this trick.

An interrupted story line makes you tune back in to wrap up the thought next time. And you don't turn the show off or close the book when you have the answer to that cliff hanger. That momentum just launches you into the next episode or chapter. And the next thing you know, it's three in the morning. This, my friends, is how a Netflix binge happens.

How can you use this on your current project?

You can enter all the paperwork except one page into your spreadsheet. Or leave the last thought, paragraph, or sentence in your document half finished. Or put the first coat of paint on all but one wall of your dining room. Imagine walking into that dining room the next day. Would you pause to think about what to do next or put off the project for a week. No! A half-painted room would nag at you until you finished it.

Now, without a doubt this made our job site a little messier sometimes. We might arrive on Saturday morning to one last water pipe lying in the middle of the kitchen floor. Or maybe the staircase was all stained except the bottom stair. Or two lightbulbs were left out of a light fixture. And you can imagine how this left me feeling a little unsatisfied some evenings when I quit a project early. But the powerful pull of that mental wiggle got me out there the next day. And finishing that final board, brick, tile, or pipe gave me the boost to launch into the next difficult thing. Then I just kept going.

I'll be honest, you'll feel some resistance to doing this at first, because your brain's push to finish things is powerful. Everything in you will be itching to reach a more natural stopping point. But when your project needs a strong chain of motivation to carry you through, you definitely want to quit early on purpose. Once you start seeing the benefits of this natural momentum cycle, you're going to use this trick like crazy. It's another fantastic way to use the way our brain is already set up to our advantage.

Try it. Don't allow yourself to put the finishing touches on your next task. Instead, leave just a couple steps undone. Then watch how you're pulled back into action immediately the next day. Get into the habit of creating this automatic starting point and you'll have a lot less downtime and reach your finish line on time.

As the schoolboys stuck on their island learned, starting a fire with two sticks is hard but once you get it started, it's easier to keep going. Use the Ovsiankina effect to pull you straight into your first step of the day and you'll start every day ahead of schedule.

You've got this. It's one of my favorite special effects. Start every day on time, and quit early.

CHAPTER ELEVEN

Troubleshooting

START BY STARTING. - MERYL STREEP

Even after I learned a lot about procrastination and using these how-to video strategies to get myself up and moving, I still sometimes found that either my progress was too slow or the work felt like too much of a grind. Those problems didn't mean my strategy wasn't working, it only meant that I'd gone off script a little bit and needed a little help to get back on track.

I paid attention to what worked for me and why. This chapter will help when you're having trouble staying in the groove. First, let's look at three troubleshooting ideas for when your progress feels too slow. I have so much to say about each of them, but I know you're ready to wrap this up and get moving on your goal so I'll do my best to be short and to the point.

Solutions For Slow Progress

Measure Your Progress

Anyone who has sold cookie dough for a new school playground or chocolate bars for band uniforms or has donated blood or given to a hospital charity drive knows the power of a well-displayed goal thermometer. They may feel a little cheesy, but watching the bars grow as you reach closer and closer to your goal feels good. Not only can people running this fundraiser see a visual representation of the progress, but everyone donating can see the colorful bar rise when they hit "send" on their donation.

There's a very good reason you see these fundraising thermometers everywhere. They work.

Yes, I'm going to tell you to create one for yourself. It doesn't have to be an exact representation of that thermometer. (But it can be.) It could simply be a circled date on the calendar when you'll take the staff or the family out to dinner if you've hit your goals for that quarter. It could be a new piece of office equipment that will make the next part of the project more fun or easier. It doesn't matter very much what it is—what matters is that before you begin your project you establish the thing and the date or event that will signal its completion.

This is one situation where you definitely can't make the rules up as you go. And you may not realize it yet, but you already know why.

It's because of dopamine.

Scheduling milestone markers throughout your project is a way to actually schedule a dopamine release. That means it's a way to schedule a motivational boost. And if you strategically set up these boosts after an exceptionally difficult segment of your project, you will increase motivation on both sides of that milestone marker.

You can have more than one win in your project. In fact, you should have more than one win. Build this right into your plan.

Aside from the dopamine release at the milestones, a visual representation of your goal progress will also be a constant reminder that even though the work feels slow, you're moving in the right direction. But uh-oh, what if you make the charts, set up the mile marker, and the needle isn't moving in the right direction?

No worries. That's why I have more than one trick up my troubleshooting sleeve.

Vuja De

You've heard of deja vu, right? (pronounced DAY-zhah-VOO) When you suddenly have the feeling that you've been in an exact situation before, even though you know that couldn't possibly be true. This is usually a very detailed moment, like you're walking down the street in Dallas in the rain and someone with a yellow umbrella walks by, and your best friend turns to you and laughs while you take a sip of your coffee from a purple cup.

Instantly you say, "This is so weird. I swear this exact thing happened before." Even though you've never been in Dallas with this friend or sipped coffee from a purple cup in the rain. Still, you'd swear it's a memory, and that makes it feel eerie.

There are a lot of theories about why this happens to us, but no definite explanation. The word itself comes from French and means already seen. Weird, huh? But we're going to turn this into something twice as weird. We're going to flip the meaning backwards.

The opposite of deja vu, is just a rearranging of the meaning and the letters until we get vuja de. (pronounced VOO-zhah-DAY) And the new rearranged meaning is such a fun concept that just saying the word makes me smile.

Vuja de is when you've seen a thing many times before, but suddenly it looks like something brand new. Make sense? It's seeing something familiar in a brand-new way.

Picture this: You're walking down the main street of the town you currently live in. You've walked down this street a hundred times before. You turn a corner at the same time of day with the same people you've done this with before, but just like that you see it in a new way.

Maybe after months and months of looking through real estate listings for a new business location, you turn that corner and see the same little vacant coffee shop you've been seeing for months, and suddenly you realize something new, that vacant shop right there is EXACTLY where you should put your new business, or that apartment is where you want to live, or that restaurant is where we should hold our next event or—you get the idea. Something strikes you and you wonder "how did I not see this before?"

If you're feeling like the progress on your project is too slow, you might just be missing something obvious that's right in front of you. This happens when we're tired, focused too heavily on one element of our project, or just plowing forward on auto-pilot. It can also happen when you're doing something so new that every task and tool is brand new to you.

Create an intentional vuja de scenario by inviting someone to take a look at the project with you. Preferably someone who knows absolutely nothing at all about the type of project you're doing. Bring a librarian to the construction site, or a doctor to the bank. Create a real fish-out-of-water scenario and see the tools and work through their eyes. Even if the project is digital, you can talk someone through the intent and process and see what brand-new vision they bring to the table.

It's best if you do this with a real human, but if for whatever reason that's not possible, just walk through it in your head. Invite an imaginary person from 1890 to walk through your high-tech smart house idea. Or an interior decorator to review your website layout.

Think of it as how it feels to revisit a place from childhood as an adult, like your old elementary school. Everything looks so much smaller and less dramatic. You understand the purpose of so many things differently than you used to.

If you're stuck in a rut, taking a moment to look at the same-old, same-old in a brand-new way can launch your project forward at record speed. Vuja de that project!

Substitution

Even after I learned a lot more about procrastination and the press play effect, and after I understood how to use this system to get myself up and moving, this procrastination habit kept sneaking up on me. You'll definitely catch your brain trying to trick you with this one so I want to make sure you can identify and stop your sneaky inner self.

By now you'll recognize when you freeze up or even when your brain sends you running from scary, difficult tasks. You'll even recognize when you're hiding away from your project with things that have zero value like watching Netflix or scrolling through social media. These habits are obvious, and you'd never argue if someone suggested you were procrastinating.

We do a pile of things that are a lot more difficult to identify as procrastination though. I call these substitutions. These distractions look so helpful at first glance that you might not even realize you shouldn't be doing them. These are things like cleaning out your email, doing a workout, or reading a business book.

Inarguably, these are really useful, positive things that you can usually feel good about doing. But even a very good thing can be used in a bad way if you are substituting it for the work toward your goal.

Here's a way to test if what you're doing is a substitution. If the thing you're doing is not taking you any closer to your goal, but it is taking up time on your calendar that is supposed to be dedicated to your goal, then it's a substitution. And that means that you, my friend, are procrastinating.

It doesn't matter if the grout is dirty or your desk drawer is messy. That's not what you're supposed to be doing right now. Substituting one of these usually positive tasks is a reaction to how scary your goal is right now, which makes it part of your F3 response.

What I'm saying is, step away from the vacuum.

This is such a common behavior that people sometimes announce their substitutions. They shrug and say something like, "Well I didn't hit my writing word count today, but I tripled scored on my activity tracker by walking 14 miles!" Or, "No I didn't finish that report, but my calendar is organized for the next 16 months!"

I mean, there must be some good in these actions, right? Who in the world can fault you for exercise?

Me. I can. And you will too from now on. Because the only way to reach your goal is to create a schedule with strict deadlines and stick to them. The only way to keep achieving goals is to be the type of person who does what you say you're going to do. So, if my calendar says I'm supposed to write, or drive to the post office, or schedule an uncomfortable meeting with my team, and instead I'm walking loops around the neighborhood to double my steps, this is not a positive or efficient use of my time and I won't meet my deadlines.

If I'm not doing what I'm supposed to be doing during goal time, then I'm procrastinating. It's that simple.

If you genuinely need more time for your workout routine, schedule that. But don't substitute your workout or anything else into the time you were supposed to be working toward your goal.

That's procrastination.

"I didn't finish this but I did finish that!" I've heard this so many times. I've even said it myself. But now I realize that by definition procrastination is anything you do that's avoiding the thing you should be doing. That's right, *anything*, not just the negative things.

When you set a goal, and day after day you're not making progress, you're going to feel bad about yourself. This causes stress because you know you can do better. Relieve that stress by taking control of your substitution habit. I say habit because we tend to go back to the same easy wins. Why? Well, you remember dopamine. We get some of that for cleaning the rug, so despite wasting our goal time, we feel good.

Recognize these substitutions. When they pop up—and I guarantee they will—take note of what sent you running off to do this easier thing. And while it was crafty of your brain to substitute a positive thing, don't accept this. Redirect yourself back to what you're supposed to be doing.

You can see how quickly we fall behind on things by substitution and how frustrating it is if you look back at your day and it looks from the surface like you were doing all kinds of good things and still not getting anywhere.

At the beginning of every week, evaluate each item on your to-do list to confirm that it's either essential (paying your bills, doing your taxes, grocery shopping), or that it's leading to completing your goal. Look back at the last week too and identify those times when substitution procrastination tripped you up.

Solutions For the Grind

Temptation Bundling

Sometimes, the thing stealing all the fun from your goal is just plain hard work. Reaching for goals of all sizes can stretch your comfort zone, your work hours, and exhaust you with the endless work grind. This doesn't mean you don't want your goal badly enough or that you're doing anything wrong. But it does mean that altering a few simple processes can improve the way you feel about every step toward your goal.

You know how much I like to use the way our brains are already set up to create a success strategy. And temptation bundling is another one of these. We're going to use this process to tackle something that you're sick and tired of doing, or maybe you never liked this part of the project from the start. If you don't create a way to enjoy these tough parts, then procrastination will eventually slow you down or end this project for good. And that's not acceptable.

Temptation bundling is all about pairing a task you really enjoy with a task you don't. You've heard this before from me and you'll hear it again. This works because it takes advantage of the way your brain works.

For example, only allow yourself to listen to a favorite music playlist when you're sorting email. This makes sorting email a lot more fun by associating it with a positive mood. Or maybe you only watch your favorite new Netflix obsession when you're working out. Or get a pedicure while you read technical documents. Only listen to a favorite podcast or audiobook when cleaning house, chopping vegetables for healthy snacks, or doing yard work.

Temptation bundling is a really effective way to create habits.

When you're thinking of a few tasks you might pair together, make sure the items you combine don't compete with each other. Combining two activities that require activity from the same part of your brain won't work any better than combining tasks that require the same part of your body. Answering emails while listening to a podcast is as useless as combining a pedicure with riding an exercise bike. They just aren't compatible. They'll crash into each other in your brain and you won't get anything out of either one.

I probably don't need to mention this, but also make sure you're not sabotaging one goal to achieve another. For example, eating a Snickers bar as you answer emails will definitely get you through the emails, but it'll probably be a setback to your healthy eating goals.

The temptation bundling strategy is different from a bribe or reward system, because the tasks happen simultaneously. And that's super important because of how our brain works, specifically with the release of dopamine. Dopamine isn't only released when we complete a task, it also shows up when we do things we really like. This means you're getting double the bang for your buck with temptation bundling.

You feel better about doing a yucky task, one you usually avoid, because now you get to do something you like right along with it. And you get a dopamine boost from your brain, which makes you feel even better and softens your dislike of the task. The dopamine also puts your brain in a state where it can more easily form new connections. You learn faster and develop habits more quickly when dopamine is floating around up here.

This combination accelerates your progress toward your goal, and all by working with instead of fighting against the way your brain already works. It's like procrastination-proofing your goal.

This strategy is especially useful when you're starting something brand new because it solidifies a new habit. That's because dopamine actually stimulates the creation of new neurons, which gets your brain ready for learning and creating new connections.

Use this. It's really one of the most useful tools you'll find, and study after study shows it's an effective way to launch into a new routine.

Pause, Rewatch, and Do-Over

One of the important ways that how-to videos pull you in is by lowering the stakes and pressure. Instead of an intimidating public lesson by a top expert, you get to watch an ordinary person tackling something you might not expect them to do. This setting immediately relaxes you into believing you also are the type of person who could tackle that thing. But we haven't talked yet about one of the most important reasons you believe that's true. It's all about the privacy.

By private, I don't mean secret, because we've already chatted about the importance of declaring your goal.

(Remember, I have a massive concrete sign in my yard that declares to the mailman and the whole world that I'm a writer.) What I mean by private, is that you're able to view the instruction in a place where you're comfortable and possibly even alone. You watch at home, in your office, or at your work site. All places where you feel some level of confidence. Now let's take that a step further.

When you're watching alone and you need a minute to mentally catch up, or google what that word even means, or how much that tool costs, or where to buy a supply you've never heard of, you just hit pause. The stakes are low. The pressure is low. You don't have to keep up in real time. Pause whenever you want and for as long as you want.

Or maybe the video shows a step you're uncertain about. Something you're sure would be simple to other people but for whatever reason you feel uncomfortable. When you're alone, you can watch that video over and over again until your confidence grows.

Maybe even when you charge forward and give it a shot, things don't really work out. But if you're tackling this project in private, who's gonna know? You can try again without feeling weird about it at all. If you just tried making banana nut bread for the first time but accidentally left out the sugar, you can quietly scrape that disgusting bread into the trash or the dog dish, and go again. Luna the lab has your back. Nobody's gonna know.

This ability to pause, rewatch, and do-over changes everything about how we approach a project. It lowers the stakes simply by displaying that the worst case scenario isn't all that bad. In fact, for Luna the lab, a do-over is downright tasty.

Building a low-stakes mindset into your project isn't difficult at all. In fact, just pausing to remind yourself how low the stakes are for a do-over, or that no one is really going to judge you for a rewatch or pause, instantly lowers the stakes and gets you moving.

If the endless hard grind of your project is pulling you down, there's a really good chance you've inflated the stakes. Remember that you can pause, rewatch, and do-over as many times as you want. If you're really struggling with this, take a quick look back at our special effects.

Each one of these effects carefully accesses a different part of the systems in your mind that are designed to lower the stakes and get you moving. Pause, rewatch, and do-over as many times as you need to. Keep the end goal in your sights, and take the next step forward.

Have Fun on Purpose

The idea of commanding ourselves to have more fun seems a little ridiculous, but hear me out on this one. It's not only possible, it's essential.

When you're having fun, your stress hormones are lower which makes you less likely to get sick, and you'll sleep better, eat better, and have more energy. These are already a bunch of great ways that you'd like your life to change, but there's more.

Your memory improves when you're having fun. You're more creative too. Which means your projects will be more likely to be filled with innovative ideas that will succeed.

Reducing your stress levels by having fun will spread creative ideas to new areas of your mind. Having more fun has not only a psychological effect, but a physiological effect too. Fun changes your mind and body all for the better.

Fun is also the most important motivation tool we have. Fun and curiosity are why we reach for the rattle that our mom shakes over our crib, why we get up to run after the family dog. Games we find fun build our muscles on the playground, funny jokes stretch our mind, and a million other games, Legos, erector sets, dolls and toys teach us important things about the world and set us up for success.

Finding fun is literally our biggest driver and most important motivator. So why, as we become adults, do we suddenly become so serious? Why do we push all the fun things into smaller portions of our lives until the only time left for it is a couple week nights and part of every other Saturday?

Seriously, why are we so serious?

Stop viewing fun as the opposite of work. It's actually fuel for more effective work. That makes injecting more fun into your work hours the secret to success. This isn't some pie-in-the-sky wishful thinking. You did this as a little kid, and you still can.

There is a really simple way to sprinkle an appropriate amount of fun into the steps toward your goal so you can have more fun more of the time. Simply incorporate more things into your day that feel playful. Things that make you smile. Things that give you a sense, a feeling, that life is good. Maybe you forgot what play even looks like. Let's review.

Play has loose rules. You don't only stop being so serious, you take yourself less seriously too, which means you'll put lower stakes on each step—an important result we were shooting for in every single one of our special effects.

The same thing happens in each of our brains when we're having fun. It doesn't matter if you're an opera singer or a football player. Whether you're using your toes every morning to find your mark on stage or to kick a ball, your brain is giving you the same chemical reward for your success. You've simply found different triggers.

If you're still stumped at what fun would look like in your current goal pursuit, think back to when you were a kid and identify the types of things that were most fun for you. I'm not asking you to add Matchbox cars or Barbie time to your schedule, but you can use the way you played with those things to root out on a foundational level what type of thing triggers your definition of fun.

Maybe you'll discover that you enjoyed setting up your games and play areas a lot more than playing the game afterward. Creating, decorating, and having a stimulating work environment are going to be part of what brings fun to your next task. Make sure your work spot is one you love. Inject that same fun into your milestone celebrations. Go all out with streamers, color coordinated snacks and T-shirts. And obviously look at where it fits in your project. Can you take a bigger hand in the creative marketing or brand design of your business?

Let's look at another type of fun. Maybe the most fun you have is watching Netflix or reading novels. (Don't do that during work hours!) What sorts of stories really grab you and pull you in? If you enjoy mysteries, then the research areas of your project may make your heart sing. If you love storytelling in general, a writing, or brand creation element of your project may be the most fun for you. Or even blogging your process and creating how-to videos of your own as you go.

I'm not into math, not at all. But if math, numbers, measurements, and statistics really make you smile, you may get into a more technical system to mark your progress. Think video game style, and create a progress bar, health status, and even points for wins along the way.

No matter what your fun triggers are, something as simple as using bright colors can signal our brain that it's fun time. It's like an open door with an invitation to come out and play a while. Use brightly colored folders, highlighters, and even colorful office furniture. Hang inspirational art that brightens the walls and your mood.

Challenge yourself or your entire team with a ticking timer. Turn on some music. Serve a glass of wine at Monday's lunch and learn.

Every single project brings layers of complex stages that require all sorts of different talents, and those layers give us infinite opportunities to inject fun at every level. Adding fun elements to your work day may sound like a very small thing, but the way this alters your body and mind has a profound effect on not only your project, but your daily experience while you reach for the goal.

When you set up your projects so they complement the way your brain works, you get more done. Which is fantastic. But even more important than that, you will enjoy every element of life more, and so will everyone you work with and live with.

Having more fun in your everyday work and life will create a ripple effect of success.

Troubleshooting Success

Align your target and strategy with your actual brain function. We're not inventing new neuropathways. We're not engaging in a battle with your psychology or energy level or anything that makes you, you. We're just tapping into the well-worn brain pathways to aim them at your targets.

Identify your project milestones early so you can celebrate your progress. Look for brand new ways to see old things. Figure out where you're craftily substituting tasks that end up slowing your progress. Then you can bundle tempting things that you like with the hardest steps. Your stakes will feel a little lower so you give yourself permission to pause, rewatch, or do-over any time you need to. And most importantly, insert the things that bring you the most joy in life through every stage of your project. Reaching the smallest and largest goals you set isn't meant to be the worst part of life. Working toward things you want is meant to be the best part of life and having fun along the way is your biggest reward.

You showed up here because you think you should be somewhere or something you're not. And you're not going to wait for something magical to just happen and change that, or for some hero to sweep in and save you. You're not expecting someone else to push you forward.

That hero, that big change you've been waiting for? It's you. And your brain already holds all the tools you need to reach your goal.

CHAPTER TWELVE

Your Goal Play Button

THE WORST THING YOU CAN DO IS NOTHING. - THEODORE ROOSEVELT

YouTube didn't begin the way you think it did. The founders didn't set up and launch some seamless business knowing that more than half of the videos would end up instructing us how to do things. Maybe they should have, since they were so DIY right from the start that their early employees were handed sealed IKEA boxes and told to put their own desks together. But they honestly never saw their company's meteoric rise coming.

They never imagined I'd build a house, John Magiro Wangare would create a power plant, Paen Long would build a plane, and they certainly never imagined that Mac would drive himself and his sister to McDonalds because of the videos shared by users on their platform. In fact, the very first YouTube video was all about elephants. And the platform itself was initially intended as a dating service—for humans, not elephants.

Steve Chen, Chad Hurley, and Jawed Karim incorporated YouTube on February 14, 2005 (Valentine's Day). They set a small goal, one they thought they might hit, and that's why for the first week, YouTube was a dating platform. The idea that they could create a site to host all the videos on the internet felt way too big and scary to them at the time. But after that first slow week as a dating platform, they pivoted and started focusing on an easy way to share videos on the internet.

The first video ever uploaded was titled, *Me at the Zoo*. The low-quality 18-second clip shows Karim at the San Diego Zoo. He says, "All right, so here we are in front of the elephants. The cool thing about these guys is that they have really, really, really long trunks, and that's, that's cool. And that's pretty much all there is to say."

This video is still available, and worth a watch.

And even though it wasn't even a thing yet, these guys were already using how-to video strategy in perfect form.

You had a young team of people who felt stuck with the options available to them. They had plenty of insecurity with their F3 responses pushing them to shoot for smaller, more achievable goals. But they could see a solution so clearly, that they could taste it. So, they took a quick and easy first step in front of some elephants. And then they did it again.

They didn't know what step 4 or step 704 of their process would look like, and they didn't have to. They took one step, then one more, and then another. They said very clearly, "We had no idea how to do it."

And then they did it anyhow.

It wasn't long before they were the biggest and most popular platform on the internet. And very quickly, how-to videos grew to dominate the site. The reason we watch these videos isn't just because we want to know how to do things. We watch the videos and execute every step for things we had no intention of doing before we watched the video. These videos don't just help us to do things, they get us to do things.

Let that sink in.

These videos don't just help us to do things, they get us to do things.

That distinction is the foundation of the press play effect. Understanding it helps you understand your own human mind, because the video format was organized to influence your minds. Learning to use the same techniques for your personal projects helps you to reach a greater potential than we ever believed was possible.

How-to videos are the perfect summary of how our brains are inspired to take action. All you have to do is press play and you're off to the races. The press play effect has forever changed how I understand my own mind, and how I create my own goal play button to successfully reach for every single goal.

Now you know how to put this into practice too. You're ready to take the first step toward your goal, and you can quickly and easily set that up.

Be Committed

In Ancient Greece, a man named Demosthenes became one of the greatest speakers of all time. He wasn't the sort of person anyone would have expected be become a great speaker. He was sick so often that he was short of breath a lot, and he also had a stammer which took a huge toll on his confidence. But he had a lot of big thoughts and was committed to sharing them.

Demosthenes set a goal of becoming a great speaker. He studied long hours to make sure his ideas were strong, and he studied great speakers to learn how to present his ideas. Then he began training with an actor so he could control his movements to make him look more confident. But still, he had a stammer and overcoming it wouldn't be easy.

He built an exercise routine where he could practice shouting his speeches while running uphill. He walked along the seashore and belted his speeches into the crashing waves. He rehearsed with pebbles in his mouth to overcome his stammer.

And when he started going out so often with friends that the progress he made toward reaching his goal slowed to a crawl, he shaved all the hair off one side of his head to make himself look so ridiculous that he'd want to stay at home and stay focused.

Demosthenes was born in 384 BCE, but we know his name today as one of the most compelling speakers of all time because of his commitment to his goal.

Way back in the hills of Ancient Greece, this hopeful man set an impossible goal and then he followed the same effective steps that we see in how-to videos today. Setting his steps up in that particular way gave him the confidence to take action without needing to understand every step of the process first. Thousands of years later, Dashrath Manjhi used the same steps to chisel a 360-foot-long path through a mountain, and an eight-year-old boy used them to drive himself to McDonalds.

Each of these people felt every bit as stuck as you feel. And each of them got unstuck.

I remember before we built our house when I knew things were really not good for my kids and me. Even though I knew I was the only one who could make things better, I kept procrastinating. I made long mental lists of reasons why it wasn't a good time, or I wasn't ready yet, or I didn't have the money, skill, courage, or whatever.

I knew that I was procrastinating. I could have told you that out loud, but I thought of procrastination as something that was happening to me. As an outside force out to sabotage my potential, my goals, my future. Something I had to fight against. And I was losing that fight.

But then I realized the enemy I had set myself up to fight was my own brain. And that not only my brain but all of our brains were designed to work this way. And instead of looking for some way to cure myself and the whole world, I decided there had to be a way to work with the systems inside my head. Other people were successfully starting and finishing big goals over and over again, and that had to mean I could use my brain to do the same thing.

It could have taken me decades to figure out how to do that. But I live in a time where the perfect system for getting unstuck just fell in my lap in the form of an accidental lemon Bundt cake.

That cake changed my life, and I hope it changed yours, too. (Remember that the next time someone tries to convince you that dessert can't be life changing.)

At a time when you felt completely stuck, too paralyzed to get yourself out of a single one of the problems you were facing, this book gave you a shove toward the first step of whatever project or goal you should be springing up to work on right now.

That's a pretty big deal.

You know your life can be better than it is today. You know you're capable of so much more. And now that you have the best psychological methods and tricks tucked in your tool belt, you're one small step away from your biggest success.

You can reach every small goal you set, and the biggest, most impossible goal you can imagine. You can set these up in a way that uses the pathways already built into your brain. And you don't even have to shave half of your head to do it.

You have the grit. You have the guts. You have the determination. And now you have a trick or two up your sleeve to get past the hardest moments.

It's official. You have everything it takes to reach your goals.

Are you ready to take the first step?

All you have to do is press play.

Quick Reference

Create Your Own Press Play Effect

A JOURNEY OF A THOUSAND MILES MUST BEGIN WITH A SINGLE STEP. - LAO TZU

Set the Scene

In order to reach your goal, you have to see it. This crystal clear visual of your end result should be so real in your mind that you feel like you could step right into it. Visualize every physical detail, and exactly what you'll feel like when you're living your goal.

Setting the scene is the first and most important move you'll make. The pull a goal exerts on you when you've set it up right is irresistible. Not only will you be eager to take the first step, nothing could hold you back.

This powerful visualization of your end result is always

essential and always first. Set the scene in your mind's eye with so much detail that you can imagine biting into that cheeseburger, lighting up your power plant, or walking through your pizza restaurant, finished home, new business, or freshly landscaped back yard.

Seeing is more than believing. Seeing leads to success.

Blind Action

This is the thing we're all here for, right? That first action step that gets you unstuck.

Leap in quickly with a simple blind action that gets things moving. Remember, I didn't have to know how to build an entire house in order to start building a house. I didn't let what I didn't know yet stop me from starting, and what you don't know yet shouldn't stop you, either. You can start right now. Just make sure this step is simple enough to quickly understand and execute. This early step forward is a commitment that changes your identity from a person who is planning to do this someday to the person who is already moving toward the goal.

Your simple success at the beginning of your project will change everything. You will feel an instant confidence boost that will carry through the project. Taking this action will make you feel bold enough to figure out the next step without feeling like you have to understand the entire process first. Move quickly into this first blind action step and you'll be released from the loop of feeling stuck.

You don't have to know how to do the whole thing in order to move one step forward.

UNSTUCK

With that quick and simple step forward, you're unstuck.

Rewind

During the most difficult parts of your project, every step can feel as hard as the first step. To avoid feeling stuck again, return to the first step.

Flash all the way back to your set up and fully visualize that final goal. And then take another single step forward. Create a physical representation and written reminders of your goal to solidify the reality of what you're about to achieve. Then keep figuring out each step until you reach the finish line.

Special Effects

The Worst Case Scenario

When analysis paralysis strikes, this little reality check will get you back on track. Ask yourself, "What's the worst case scenario here?" And make sure you stick to the scenarios that are actually likely to happen. Guessing that you could be struck by a meteor is off the table.

Nearly every time you ask this question, the answer is that if you do it wrong, you'll have to do it over. And that's a scenario you can easily live with. Now you can leap in with no worries.

If your worst case scenario reveals that you need more safety precautions or research, do that quickly and get back out there. The worst case scenario effect lowers your stakes so you can reach your goal quickly.

The Yet Principle

When you end every "I can't" or "I don't know how" with the word yet, everything changes. You instantly become the sort of person who starts something before you know how to do it. You learn on the job. This system ends up being way more efficient and effective than spending years researching a project, because you can't possibly know which data is most relevant until you get your hands dirty.

If you only do the types of projects that you know how to do, then the best you can hope for is to stay where you are. And you're definitely not the type of person who stays still.

Approach every step of your project with the powerful idea that, "I don't know how yet, but give me a minute and I'll figure it out."

The Last Person on Earth

Nothing encourages a creative brainstorm like a quick last person on earth scenario. If you were the last person on earth, could you figure out some way to achieve the thing in front of you?

This playful thought gives you a broader playbook and eliminates the artificial constraints we put on our thoughts.

When you're stuck and don't have a single idea how to begin the step in front of you, prod your mind toward a creative solution with this smart mental game.

The Quit Early Effect

You can intentionally set off a motivation chain in your own mind. All you have to do is plan an interruption near the end of a task so your brain will insist you get back out and finish it the next day. Creating an irresistible starting point is the best way to keep motivation high, especially during the toughest parts of your project.

Just like an addictive video game, quitting early creates a loop of motivation and action that will take you all the way to your finish line.

Troubleshooting

No matter how perfectly you set up your project, big goals bring unexpected road blocks. Thankfully, we already have a system built in to our brains to overcome even the most frustrating challenges.

When your progress feels slow, set up a measurement system so your milestones are met with an energizing dopamine burst. Look at the same-old, same-old in a brand new way by using a little vuja de in your project. And when you're working all day on good things but not inching closer to your goal, check your goal for substitutions. Learn to recognize this sneaky form of procrastination so it can't drag you down.

If the difficult grind of your project has you physically and mentally exhausted, try temptation bundling by attaching a favorite task to a boring one. Lower the pressure and stakes of your next step by giving yourself permission to pause, rewind, and do-over as needed. Finally, and most importantly, build fun things into every stage of your project on purpose. The benefits of fun alter your body and mind for a profoundly positive effect on your project and your life.

In Summary

The three simple steps of how-to video strategy are the secret to getting up and moving on any goal of any size. This works for every single person everywhere. This system is perfectly represented and optimized in the how-to videos we've gotten so used to seeing on YouTube, TikTok, Instagram and dozens of other platforms.

How-to videos did not invent this system.

Successful people throughout history have used the same techniques in the same order to reach their goals. This system works because it's perfectly aligned with the way our brains are already set up to work.

Now, for the first time in history these videos give us unlimited examples of how to optimize this system and use it for the best results. There's never been an easier time to get unstuck. But with so many distractions and so much information coming from different directions, it can be difficult to narrow down the exact steps you need to get from here to your goal. And that's why I put it all down in this book. Because I was as stuck as you are.

How-to videos got me unstuck. And now in the true DIY nature of our times, you can use the exact same system to get yourself unstuck.

So, what are you waiting for?

All you have to do is press play.

Lemon Bundt Cake Recipe

This recipe got me moving. After you eat it, you better get moving too, because you have calories to work off. It's worth it.

Ingredients

1 cup (2 sticks) softened unsalted butter
3 cups all-purpose flour
2 tablespoons grated lemon zest
1/3 cup fresh lemon juice
1 teaspoon baking soda
1 teaspoon salt
2 cups granulated sugar
6 large eggs
1 cup sour cream

Directions

Step 1
Preheat your oven to 350 F. Spray flour baking spray into a 12-cup Bundt pan or butter and flour it. Whisk flour, baking soda, salt, and lemon zest together in a medium bowl.

Step 2
In a separate bowl beat butter and sugar together until light and fluffy. (About four minutes.) Add eggs one at a time, beating the mixture well after each egg. Add lemon juice and mix well.

Step 3

Turn mixer to low and slowly add half of flour just until blended. Add sour cream. Then mix in the other half of the flour just until it's blended. Don't overdo the mixing at this stage. It's fine if everything around you is covered in flour. That's how I do it too. Spoon your mixture you're your greased and floured pan and tap the pan on your counter to level and release air pockets.

Step 4

Bake 50-60 minutes. A toothpick inserted in center should come out clean. Cool in the pan for 30 minutes, then remove and cool completely on a rack.

Optional: Mix 1.5-2 tablespoons of lemon juice with 1 cup powdered sugar for a glaze.

Not optional: Serve with coffee.

Acknowledgements

When I was sixteen, my dad took me to a café-style mom and pop restaurant in rural Wisconsin. We had little disposable income, so eating in a restaurant was a big deal that happened maybe two or three times a year. I had enormous expectations for that meal, and in order to really get the most of the experience dad and I had both skipped lunch.

I can still remember exactly what I ordered: Country slab pork chops with mashed potatoes and Grandma's buttered sweetcorn.

I imagined my own grandma's phenomenal cooking while we waited, my stomach growling and mouth-watering. Dad stretched back in his seat, picked up a white and blue checked linen napkin and held it up between us with a distant look in his eyes. "I bet this was less than a dollar, and just look at it." He ran the satin-stitched edge through his fingers.

It wasn't the first time he had gone through a ritual like this, so I knew what was coming.

He continued, "Someone had to plant the seed, grow the fiber, harvest it, turn it into thread, weave it, dye it, sew it, ship it to a store, sell it to a wholesaler, until it finally ended up here. How many hands do you think this passed through before it landed here? How do they do all this and still make a profit everywhere along the way?" He shook his head, eyes alight.

My dad was forever serving up moments like this. He was filled with pure, unabashed wonder and generous side helpings of curiosity.

The way he marveled over the tiniest details of the tiniest things taught me the most important life lesson: to be grateful for even the small, simple things. And that's what this acknowledgements section is all about. The dozens of hands my ideas, stories and research passed through during the four years I researched and wrote this book.

Before I name names though, I have to tell you about the country slab pork chops and buttered sweetcorn, because to this day that remains the most disappointing meal I've ever been served in my life.

My entire serving of corn—straight from a can—fit on my spoon in a single bite. I had actual tears running down my face when my fork stuck straight up in my solidified scoop of potatoes. But they were the laughter kind of tears, not the crying ones. Because Dad just couldn't stop the jokes.

He poked at my pork chop and said, "My little pink piglet on the farm got hurt worse than that sneaking under the fence."

We ate that terrible food, and then dad paid the bill without complaint. He put his arm around me as we walked to the car, smiled and said, "We're making memories."

And obviously we were, because I've been in a thousand restaurants since that day but can't remember a single meal as clearly as that one. The lessons from that day are still crystal clear too. Not just being grateful, which is huge, but also that even when things are going terribly wrong or are incredibly difficult, laughing through the challenge changes everything.

Twenty years later my kids and I laughed through the worst parts of building a house, all the while marveling at the details.

Special thanks to my dad, Bruce Puttkammer, for passing his sense of wonder on to me and therefore directly into this book. And also to my grandparents George Puttkammer and Doris Freemore for raising him with this trait. They passed the laughter on to my Auntie Darlene too, and she shared it with my Uncle Bobby. Their fingerprints are throughout my life.

My mom, Virginia Barrette, was a therapist and would have loved every bit of the research and stories here. I miss her every day, but I also see how each part of my life and this book still pass through her hands.

Four years of research, planning, and writing may sound like plenty, but the true measure of those hours increases exponentially when you include the time people in my life contributed in shared stories, debates, psychology journals, and real time social experiments—sometimes conducted formally, but often over dinner and a glass of wine.

Thank you, Larry Middleton, for nodding along enthusiastically with the first and the hundredth time I said, "I read the craziest thing today."

Thanks to Sandy Marshall and Anita Middleton-Keller for the hugs and encouragement when my eyes where bleary from late nights at the keyboard. And thanks to Adele Holmes for the author-to-author support, and to Mari Farthing for yet another stellar editing job. It turns out, working with great friends is a fine thing to do.

By now you know my kids well because they have generously allowed me to share the strangest parts of their lives. But you should also know that Hope, Kei, Drew, Jada, and Roman continue to support my crazy ideas and even have a direct hand in book related things like research, edits, and cover brainstorms. And as you saw in the dedication, Hope is my business partner so the number of times each element of this book passed through her hands is bordering on ridiculous.

And finally, the first acknowledgement I've written since becoming a grandma. There is no way I can close this book without a thank you to the three little girls who make my heart smile. I'll be telling and writing stories to them for decades to come. Winry, Nora, and Virginia, keep the magic and the laughter alive, and know that I love you forever.

References

Art of the 20th Century. (2012, January 1). *Grandma Moses.* History of art: Naive art - grandma moses. Retrieved Jan 4, 2018, from http://www.all-art.org/art_20th_century/moses1.html

Aslam, S. (2022, August 14). • youtube by the numbers (2022): Stats, Demographics & Fun Facts. Omnicore Agency. Retrieved June 13, 2022, from https://www.omnicoreagency.com/youtube-statistics/

AtMigration (2015, July 15). Dashrath Manjhi: Some lesser known facts on the mountain man who worked for 22 years and carved a path through a mountain. India Today. Retrieved December 3, 2018, from https://www.indiatoday.in/education-today/gk-and-current-affairs/story/dashrath-manjhi-282520-2015-07-15

Babbel, S. (2020, October 29). Vuja de: Finding meaning after trauma. New Harbinger Publications, Inc. Retrieved December 14, 2020, from https://www.newharbinger.com/blog/self-help/vuja-de-finding-meaning-after-trauma/

Bannister, R. (2004). The four-minute mile. Lyons Press.

Bartlett, F. C. (2003). Remembering: A study in experimental and Social Psychology. Cambridge University Press.

BBC. (2017, April 13). Boy learns to drive on YouTube for McDonald's Joyride. BBC News. Retrieved April 14, 2017, from https://www.bbc.com/news/world-us-canada-39587853

Bekoff, M. (2014, May 2). The importance of play: Having fun must be taken seriously. Psychology Today. Retrieved Sept 19, 2019, from https://www.psychologytoday.com/us/blog/animal-emotions/201405/the-importance-play-having-fun-must-be-taken-seriously

Bergland, C. (2013, May 30). The secret to achieving a big goal is... Psychology Today. Retrieved July 9, 2018, from https://www.psychologytoday.com/us/blog/the-athletes-way/201305/the-secret-achieving-big-goal-is

Biles, Simone (2018). Courage to soar: A body in motion, a life in balance. ZONDERVAN.

Biography.com. (2014, April 2). Grandma moses. Biography.com. Retrieved December 4, 2018, from https://www.biography.com/artist/grandma-moses

Bloomberg, J. J., Peters, B. T., Cohen, H. S., & Mulavara, A. P. (2015). Enhancing astronaut performance using sensorimotor adaptability training. Frontiers in Systems Neuroscience, 9. https://doi.org/10.3389/fnsys.2015.00129

Boitnott, J. (2014, May 17). Dilbert's Scott Adams on why it's better to have a system than a goal ... Dilbert's Scott Adams on Why It's Better to Have a System Than a Goal. Retrieved September 23, 2019, from https://www.inc.com/john-boitnott/dilbert-s-scott-adams-on-why-it-s-better-to-have-a-system-than-a-goal.html

Bowerman, M. (2017, April 13). 8-year-old learns to drive on YouTube, heads to McDonald's. USA Today. Retrieved April 24, 2017, from https://www.usatoday.com/story/news/nation-now/2017/04/13/8-year-old-learns-drive-youtube-heads-mcdonalds/100408432/

Bryant, J. (2010). 3:59.4: The Quest to break the four-minute mile. Cornerstone Digital.

Cardone, G. (2018, July 8). Write your goals down, first thing each day. Grant Cardone - 10X Your Business and Life. Retrieved May 3, 2019, from https://grantcardone.com/write-your-goals-down-first-thing-each-day/

Carlin, G. (2008, July 8). Vuja de. YouTube. Retrieved August 30, 2018, from https://www.youtube.com/watch?v=B7LBSDQ14eA

Cerezo, A. (2020, April 10). The Tongan castaways of Ata Island: Surviving with one of The six boys. Castaway Channel RSS. Retrieved May. 3, 2020, from https://paradise.docastaway.com/six-tongan-castaways-ata-island-shipwreck-1965/

Child, J., & Prud'homme, A. (2009). My life in France. Duckworth.

Clarey, C. (2014, February 22). Olympians use imagery as mental training. The New York Times. Retrieved October 28, 2021, from https://www.nytimes.com/2014/02/23/sports/olympics/olympians-use-imagery-as-mental-training.html

Coller, P. (2017, April 12). 8-year-old E. Palestine boy drives little sister to McDonald's. WKBN.com. Retrieved May 13, 2017, from https://www.wkbn.com/news/8-year-old-e-palestine-boy-drives-little-sister-to-mcdonalds/

Craig, R. C. (1965). Discovery, task completion, and the assignment as factors in motivation. Sage Journals. Retrieved November 4, 2021, from https://journals.sagepub.com/doi/abs/10.3102/000283120

02004217

Csikszentmihalyi, M. (2009). Flow: The psychology of optimal experience. Harper and Row.

Dean, J. (2021, June 9). Zeigarnik effect: Unfinished tasks are hard to forget. PsyBlog. Retrieved December 14, 2021, from https://www.spring.org.uk/2021/06/zeigarnik-effect.php

Deccan Chronicle. (2016, May 23). Meet the man who lives on a floating island made of plastic bottles. Deccan Chronicle. Retrieved December 4, 2018, from https://www.deccanchronicle.com/lifestyle/pets-and-environment/230516/meet-the-man-who-lives-on-a-floating-island-made-of-plastic-bottles.html

Digital, G. (2021, June 21). Jim Carrey's law of attraction and visualization tips. Influencive. Retrieved August 23, 2021, from https://www.influencive.com/jim-carreys-law-of-attraction-and-visualization-tips/

Docastaway. (2020, May 20). Peter Warner | Captain who saved the six castaways boys in 1966. YouTube. Retrieved June 14, 2020, from https://www.youtube.com/watch?v=tT1C4BSRzak

Docastaway. (2021, February 8). The Tongan castaways making fire on Ata Island. YouTube. Retrieved March 27, 2021, from https://www.youtube.com/watch?v=YjdC16jxHwE

Elliot, A. J., & Harackiewicz, J. M. (1994). Goal setting, achievement orientation, and intrinsic motivation: A mediational analysis. Journal of Personality and Social Psychology, 66(5), 968–980. https://doi.org/10.1037/0022-3514.66.5.968

Escobar, S. (2021, July 15). 15 fun facts that will make you love Simone Biles even more. Good Housekeeping. Retrieved October 9, 2021, from https://www.goodhousekeeping.com/life/inspirational-stories/news/g3779/who-is-simone-biles/

EWU History. (2021, November 9). How six kids survived being shipwrecked for 15 months. YouTube. Retrieved December 16, 2021, from https://www.youtube.com/watch?v=Ph2azNQ_f5Q

Giaimo, C. (2021, June 7). The Animal Kingdom's oddest ways of handling anxiety. Atlas Obscura. Retrieved January 1, 2022, from https://www.atlasobscura.com/articles/the-animal-kingdoms-oddest-ways-of-handling-anxiety

Gill, N. S. (2019, June 3). Profile of demosthenes, the greek orator. ThoughtCo. Retrieved September, 2019, from https://www.thoughtco.com/demosthenes-greek-orator-118793

Globokar, L. (2020, March 5). The power of visualization and how to use it. Forbes. Retrieved October 11, 2020, from https://www.forbes.com/sites/lidijaglobokar/2020/03/05/t

he-power-of-visualization-and-how-to-use-it/?sh=5866dcfe6497

Golding, W., Baker, J. R., & Ziegler, A. P. (2016). William Golding's lord of the flies. Penguin.

Goldstein, E. B. (2015). Cognitive psychology: Connecting mind, research, and everyday experience. Cengage Learning.

Good News Network. (2015, March 21). The man who single-handedly carved a road through a mountain to help his village. Good News Network. Retrieved February 8, 2018, from https://www.goodnewsnetwork.org/man-single-handedly-carved-road-mountain/

Grall, V. (2018, November 2). The postman who built a palace made of Pebbles. Messy Nessy Chic. Retrieved April 14, 2019, from https://www.messynessychic.com/2013/04/16/the-postman-who-built-a-palace-made-of-pebbles/

Gravano, S., Lacquaniti, F., & Zago, M. (2021, December 3). Mental imagery of object motion in weightlessness. Nature News. Retrieved January 3, 2022, from https://www.nature.com/articles/s41526-021-00179-z

Great Big Story Podcast, D. (2018, March 6). Meet the man who built his own power plant. YouTube. Dangote. Retrieved January 17, 2019, from https://www.youtube.com/watch?v=9YrcruOIAPs

Gymnastics HQ. (2022, August 8). 10 reasons Simone Biles is so successful (numbers 5-10 you can do too!). Gymnastics HQ. Retrieved February 15, 2022, from https://gymnasticshq.com/10-reasons-simone-biles-is-so-successful/

Hardeveld, J. van. (2021, December 6). Richart Sowa: A Green Island made of plastic bottles. Greentravelife.com. Retrieved December 29, 2021, from https://greentravelife.com/richart-sowa-a-green-island-made-of-plasti-bottles/

Harkin, B., Webb, T. L., Chang, B. P., Prestwich, A., Conner, M., Kellar, I., Benn, Y., & Sheeran, P. (2016). Does monitoring goal progress promote goal attainment? A meta-analysis of the experimental evidence. Psychological Bulletin, 142(2), 198–229. https://doi.org/10.1037/bul0000025

Heires, K. (2017, September 1). Risk Management Magazine - The Psychology of Risk. Magazine. Retrieved April 18, 2019, from https://www.rmmagazine.com/articles/article/2017/09/01/-The-Psychology-of-Risk-#:~:text=The%20psychology%20of%20risk%20is,in%20the%20face%20of%20risk

Hengen, K. M., & Alpers, G. W. (2019, July 3). What's the risk? fearful individuals generally overestimate negative outcomes and they dread outcomes of specific events. Frontiers. Retrieved July 29, 2019, from

https://www.frontiersin.org/articles/10.3389/fpsyg.2019.0
1676/full

Hernandez, P. (2018, November 7). Half of YouTube viewers use it to learn how to do things they've never done. The Verge. Retrieved November 3, 2019, from https://www.theverge.com/2018/11/7/18071992/youtube-pew-study-education-news-childrens-videos

Interview, O. S. (2011, October 12). What Oprah learned from Jim Carrey. Oprah.com. Retrieved November 27, 2018, from https://www.oprah.com/oprahs-lifeclass/what-oprah-learned-from-jim-carrey-video

Jacques, E.J. (n.d.). The man who moved a Mountain. theTrumpet.com. Retrieved December 3, 2021, from https://www.thetrumpet.com/13619-the-man-who-moved-a-mountain

Jay, R. (2013, November 14). An island made from plastic bottles by Richart Sowa. YouTube. Retrieved December 24, 2021, from https://www.youtube.com/watch?v=GnLhWpy_nqI

Kandel, E. R. (2007). In search of memory: The emergence of a new science of mind. W.W. Norton & Co.

Karanja, S. (2020, June 29). High School student produces Hydro Power. Nation. Retrieved June 9, 2021, from https://nation.africa/kenya/counties/muranga/high-school-student-produces-hydro-power-902772

Karim, J. (2005, April 23). Me at the zoo. YouTube. Retrieved August 10, 2017, from https://www.youtube.com/watch?v=jNQXAC9IVRw

Karin, R., Karin Roelofs http://orcid.org/0000-0002-8863-8978 Google Scholar One contribution of 17 to a theme issue 'Movement suppression: brain mechanisms for stopping and stillness'., & Al., E. (2017, February 27). Freeze for action: Neurobiological mechanisms in animal and human freezing. Philosophical Transactions of the Royal Society B: Biological Sciences. Retrieved October 3, 2020, from https://royalsocietypublishing.org/doi/10.1098/rstb.2016.0206

Kidskonnect, T. (2022, May 20). Memory encoding: Memory processes storage & retrieval. The Human Memory. Retrieved May 23, 2022, from https://human-memory.net/memory-encoding/

Kirgiosa, E., H.Mandelb, G., YejiParkc, L.Milkmana, K., M.Grometc, D., S.Kayc, J., L.Duckworthad, A., (2020, October 15). Teaching temptation bundling to boost exercise: A field experiment. Organizational Behavior and Human Decision Processes. Retrieved October 24, 2020, from https://www.sciencedirect.com/science/article/pii/S0749597820303855X#:~:

Langreo, L. (2018, September 11). Why generation Z learners

prefer YouTube lessons over Printed Books. Education Week. Retrieved August, 2019, from https://www.edweek.org/teaching-learning/why-generation-z-learners-prefer-youtube-lessons-over-printed-books/2018/09

Lieberman, C. (2019, March 25). Why you procrastinate (it has nothing to do with self-control). The New York Times. Retrieved April 29, 2020, from https://www.nytimes.com/2019/03/25/smarter-living/why-you-procrastinate-it-has-nothing-to-do-with-self-control.html

Ling, T. (2021, May 10). The puzzling psychology of procrastination and how to stop it. How to stop procrastination, explained by a psychologist | BBC Science Focus Magazine. Retrieved December 7, 2021, from https://www.sciencefocus.com/science/procrastination/

Maddux, J. E. (2009). Self-efficacy: The Power of Believing You Can. The Oxford Handbook of Positive Psychology, 334–344. https://doi.org/10.1093/oxfordhb/9780195187243.013.0031

Makinson, R. (2021, October 28). How spanx founder Sara Blakely created a billion-dollar brand. CEO Today. Retrieved December 28, 2021, from https://www.ceotodaymagazine.com/2021/10/how-spanx-founder-sara-blakely-created-a-billion-dollar-brand/

Margaritoff, M. (2021, May 26). The inspiring true story of dashrath manjhi: The 'mountain man' who spent decades carving up Indian hillsides for better roads. All That's Interesting. Retrieved June 11, 2021, from https://allthatsinteresting.com/dashrath-manjhi

Martin, R. (2017, April 13). An 8-year-old drives himself to McDonald's. NPR. Retrieved May 5, 2017, from https://www.npr.org/2017/04/13/523709908/an-8-year-old-drives-himself-to-mcdonalds

Mascarenhas, J. A. (2015, January 23). The man who carved a road through the mountain so his people could reach a doctor in time. The Better India. Retrieved February 12, 2019, from https://www.thebetterindia.com/18326/the-man-who-moved-a-mountain-milaap-dashrath-manjhi/

Masicampo, E. J., & Baumeister, R. F. (2011). Consider it done! plan making can eliminate the cognitive effects of unfulfilled goals. Journal of Personality and Social Psychology, 101(4), 667–683. https://doi.org/10.1037/a0024192

Masterclass. (2022, August 30). Sara Blakely Bio: How the self-made billionaire invented spanx - 2022. MasterClass. Retrieved September 11, 2022, from https://www.masterclass.com/articles/sara-blakely-founder-of-spanx

Maxus357. (2021, November 22). The timeless and universal strengths of Bruce Lee's letter to himself. Medium. Retrieved December 27, 2021, from https://medium.com/@maximevilleneuve1/the-timeless-and-universal-strengths-of-bruce-lees-letter-to-himself-bddbbca17b20

McGraw, K. O., & Fiala, J. (1982, March 1). Undermining the Zeigarnik effect: Another hidden cost of reward. Wiley Online Library. Retrieved March 5, 2020, from https://onlinelibrary.wiley.com/doi/10.1111/j.1467-6494.1982.tb00745.x

McGuire, C. (2017, June 6). A man has built a working plane after watching YouTube videos about Jets. The Sun. Retrieved March 5, 2020, from https://www.thesun.co.uk/travel/3736262/a-man-has-built-a-working-plane-after-watching-youtube-videos-about-jets/

Menezes, F. (2017, September 27). Full power: Meet the ingenious Kenyan student who built a power station from scratch. BrightVibes. Retrieved March 5, 2020, from https://www.brightvibes.com/full-power-meet-the-ingenious-kenyan-student-who-built-a-power-station-from-scratch/

Mental.imagery.and.implicit.memory. (2012). Handbook of Imagination and Mental Simulation, 55–72. https://doi.org/10.4324/9780203809846-8

Milkman, K. L., Minson, J. A., & Volpp, K. G. (2014). Holding the hunger games hostage at the gym: An evaluation of temptation bundling. Management Science, 60(2), 283–299. https://doi.org/10.1287/mnsc.2013.1784

Miller, H. L. (2021, November 18). Sara Blakely: 7 life lessons from the founder of Spanx. Leaders.com. Retrieved December 1, 2021, from https://leaders.com/articles/women-in-business/sara-blakely-spanx/

Mind Help. (2022, June 16). Understanding procrastination: 6 common causes and how to stop. Mind Help. Retrieved June 24, 2022, from https://mind.help/topic/procrastination/

Moore, S. (2014, November 4). What Sara Blakely wished she knew in her 20s. Marie Claire Magazine. Retrieved December 3, 2020, from https://www.marieclaire.com/politics/news/a11508/sara-blakely-interview/

Morrissey, M. (2017, December 7). The power of writing down your goals and dreams. HuffPost. Retrieved April 3, 2019, from https://www.huffpost.com/entry/the-power-of-writing-down_b_12002348

Murphy, J. J. (2016). Demosthenes. Encyclopædia Britannica. Retrieved April 21, 2021, from https://www.britannica.com/biography/Demosthenes-Greek-statesman-and-orator

Murphy, J., & McMahan, I. (2001). The Power of Your Subconscious Mind. Bantam Books.

Murphy, M. (2018, April 15). Neuroscience explains why you need to write down your goals if you actually want to achieve them. Forbes. Retrieved March 11, 2018, from https://www.forbes.com/sites/markmurphy/2018/04/15/neuroscience-explains-why-you-need-to-write-down-your-goals-if-you-actually-want-to-achieve-them/?sh=443460ab7905

Murphy, M. (2021, September 3). Are smart goals dumb? Leadership IQ. Retrieved December 1, 2021, from https://www.leadershipiq.com/blogs/leadershipiq/35353793-are-smart-goals-dumb

Power, N. (2018). Man builds own power plant from scratch and connects electricity to his ... Man Builds Own Power Plant From Scratch And Connects Electricity To His Entire Village. Retrieved June 18, 2019, from https://www.nigeriaelectricityhub.com/2018/01/30/man-builds-own-power-plant-from-scratch-and-connects-electricity-to-his-entire-village/

Reisen, H. (2010). Louisa May Alcott: The Woman Behind Little Women. Picador.

Robertson, H. (2017, June 2). The man who built his plane using YouTube videos. BBC News. Retrieved July 1, 2019, from https://www.bbc.com/news/world-asia-39945650

Rose, D. H. (2022, June 16). The psychology of unfinished tasks. Ness Labs. Retrieved January 1, 2020, from https://nesslabs.com/unfinished-tasks

Rousseau, C., Barbiero, M., Pozzo, T., Papaxanthis, C., & White, O. (2020). Actual and imagined movements reveal a dual role of the Insular Cortex for motor control. Cerebral Cortex, 31(5), 2586–2594. https://doi.org/10.1093/cercor/bhaa376

Roy Chowdhury, M. (2019, May 2). The Science & Psychology of goal-setting 101. PositivePsychology.com. Retrieved May 29, 2020, from https://positivepsychology.com/goal-setting-psychology/

Sliwa, J. (2015). Frequently monitoring progress toward goals increases chance of success. American Psychological Association. Retrieved November 17, 2020, from https://www.apa.org/news/press/releases/2015/10/progress-goals

Slotnick, S. D., Thompson, W. L., & Kosslyn, S. M. (2005). Visual mental imagery induces retinotopically organized activation of early visual areas. Cerebral Cortex, 15(10), 1570–1583. https://doi.org/10.1093/cercor/bhi035

Smithsonian. (n.d.). Grandma moses. Smithsonian American Art Museum. Retrieved December 14, 2021, from https://americanart.si.edu/artist/grandma-moses-5826

Sowa, R. (n.d.). Spiral Island on floating bottles. Spiral Island on Floating Bottles. Retrieved January 24, 2021, from http://environment-ecology.com/habitat-world/54-spiral-island.html

Staff Editor. (2022, June 16). What is the Zeigarnik effect and how it works. Mind Help. Retrieved June 24, 2022, from https://mind.help/topic/zeigarnik-effect/

Staff. (2018, July 6). Dashrath Manjhi: The mountain man- The Inspiring & Untold Story of an unsung hero. https://www.oneindia.com. Retrieved August 16, 2018, from https://www.oneindia.com/feature/dashrath-manjhi-the-mountain-man-the-inspiring-untold-story-of-an-unsung-hero-1841887.html?story=2

Standford, B. (2018, April 17). Sara Blakely, founder and CEO, Spanx. YouTube. Retrieved March 5, 2021, from https://www.youtube.com/watch?v=TPURpzGPMxQ&t=76s

Statistic Brain. (2018, December 15). New Years resolution statistics. Statistic Brain. Retrieved October 17, 2021, from https://www.statisticbrain.com/new-years-resolution-statistics/

Sussex Publishers. (n.d.). Neuroscientists discover the roots of "fear-evoked freezing". Psychology Today. Retrieved October 17, 2021, from https://www.psychologytoday.com/us/blog/the-athletes-way/201405/neuroscientists-discover-the-roots-fear-evoked-freezing

Tae Oh, T. (2022, February 1). Setting fun goals may make you happier this year. Psychology Today. Retrieved May 30, 2022, from https://www.psychologytoday.com/us/blog/the-pursuit-fun/202202/setting-fun-goals-may-make-you-happier-year

Taylor, E. (2016, August 11). A brief encounter with Simone Biles on her way to olympic gold. Vanity Fair. Retrieved July 19, 2021, from https://www.vanityfair.com/culture/2016/08/simone-biles-olympic-gold-medal-before

Tom, S. M., Fox, C. R., Trepel, C., & Poldrack, R. A. (2007). The neural basis of loss aversion in decision-making under risk. Science, 315(5811), 515–518. https://doi.org/10.1126/science.1134239

Walker, L. (2020, August 4). #29 in my own process. Bruce Lee. Retrieved November 3, 2020, from https://brucelee.com/podcast-blog/2017/1/18/29-in-my-own-process

Walsh, M. (2018, November 16). Cambodian mechanic fearlessly chases his dream of building a working airplane. LifeDaily. Retrieved December 1, 2019, from https://www.lifedaily.com/story/cambodian-mechanic-fearlessly-chases-his-dream-building-working-airplane/

Waxman, O. B. (2016, September 7). Grandma moses day: Why she started painting at age 76. Time. Retrieved

October 12, 2019, from
https://time.com/4482257/grandma-moses-history/

White, K. (2017, April 12). Young driver gets help from YouTube. weirtondailytimes.com. Retrieved January 4, 2018, from https://www.weirtondailytimes.com/news/local-news/2017/04/young-driver-gets-help-from-youtube/

Williams, H. (2021, July 18). A real life lord of the flies: The 50-year-old story of a group of teens stranded on an Island. CBS News. Retrieved January, 2022, from https://www.cbsnews.com/news/shipwreck-deserted-island-south-pacific-survivors-60-minutes-2021-07-18/

WKBN27. (2017, April 12). 8-year-old E. Palestine boy drives little sister to McDonald's. YouTube. Retrieved June 14, 2017, from https://www.youtube.com/watch?v=bE2idwa4uY0

Wolfe, A. (2013, October 12). Sara Blakely of spanx: Smooth operator. The Wall Street Journal. Retrieved November 3, 2021, from https://www.wsj.com/articles/sara-blakely-of-spanx-smooth-operator-1381538171

Woods, T. (2022, July 22). The power of believing in yourself. Psychology Today. Retrieved February 14, 2022, from https://www.psychologytoday.com/us/blog/between-cultures/202207/the-power-believing-in-yourself

Yang, H., Stamatogiannakis, A., Chattopadhyay, A., & Chakravarti, D. (2021, October 11). Why we set unattainable goals. Harvard Business Review. Retrieved December 19, 2021, from https://hbr.org/2021/01/why-we-set-unattainable-goals

If you enjoyed *Unstuck*, then you will love…

CARA BROOKINS' REAL-LIFE STORY OF GETTING UNSTUCK

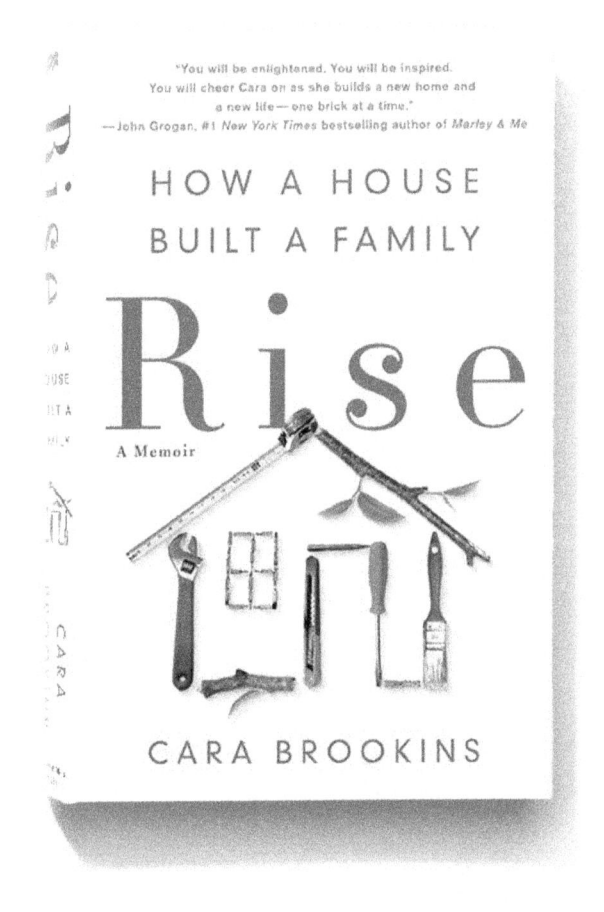

available wherever books are sold

www.ingramcontent.com/pod-product-compliance
Lightning Source LLC
LaVergne TN
LVHW090738300725
816814LV00010B/6/J